CONTENTS

QUALITY IN SECONDARY SCHOOLS AND COLLEGES SERIES

Series Editor: Clyde Chitty

This series publishes on a wide range of topics related to successful education for the 11–19 age group. It reflects the growing interest in whole-school curriculum planning together with the effective teaching of individual subjects and themes. There are also books devoted to management and administration, examinations and assessment, pastoral care strategies, relationships with parents and governors and the implications for schools of changes in teacher education. Titles include:

Valuing English

Reflections on the National Curriculum

Roger Knight

David Fulton Publishers

London

David Fulton Publishers Ltd
2 Barbon Close, London WC1N 3JX

First published in Great Britain by David Fulton Publishers 1996

Note: The right of Roger Knight to be identified as the author of this work has been asserted by him in accordance with the Copyright, Designs and Patents Act 1988.

Copyright © Roger Knight

British Library Cataloguing in Publication Data

A catalogue record for this book is available from the British Library

ISBN 1-85346-374-4

Typeset by The Harrington Consultancy Ltd
Printed in Great Britain by BPC Books and Journals Ltd., Exeter

Foreword

At the heart of this book is the firm conviction that the study of the English language and the study of its literature are inextricably connected – that 'English' cannot indeed be 'English' unless it is rooted in and unified by the study of literature. For this reason, it was a serious mistake, in the author's view, for Speaking and Listening to be split off and assessed separately from Reading and Writing in the original structure of National Curriculum English.

It is Roger Knight's strongly-held belief, articulated with great conviction and clarity in the pages that follow, that if literature is at the heart of the English curriculum, then literature will be an authentic source of standards in the teaching of English: standards in the language we observe, use and attempt to develop in young people. If the public language for the discussion of English has so far proved inadequate, this is largely because it has become detached from the sources that should have nourished it – principally English literature.

Clyde Chitty
Birmingham
March 1996

Introduction

The dust seems, for the time being, to have settled. There sits the revised National Curriculum English document, slim and supposedly more 'manageable' than its bulky forerunner, the shape of 'English' to come in the next few years: 'English', moreover, in its most public guise. The last few years have been unsettled and unsettling: acrimonious debate about the revision of the 1990 Order; the unhappy history of the Standard Attainment Tests (SATs); professional resentment at 'political' interference in matters demanding professional judgement – these have not added to the dignity of the English teaching profession or confirmed it in the public esteem. The instability of recent years has nevertheless been a provocation to thinking about 'English' and its place in education. To be an English teacher is to be a critic – and to teach others to be critics – of language. What above all has called (and will continue to call) for critical vigilance is the public language of 'English'.

There is something inherently problematic about an attempt to formulate a public language which will standardize teaching and learning in 'English': a subject in which (as, arguably, in no other) the culture, convictions and enthusiasms of individual teachers are of the essence. The public versions (the National Curriculum Orders) thus naturally challenge those who have to live by them to reflect more keenly upon their own: to ask in what degree the public versions connect with their own settled beliefs and practices. Public language and individual conviction need to be in a healthy relation to one another. We need to feel that the language in which 'official' 'English' is framed is rooted in an understanding of the subject to which we can attach ourselves, that it speaks *for* us as well as *to* us. Unless it possesses the capacity to inspire and energize those to whom it is addressed it will be null. It needs to be a generative language, able that is to generate the good practice by which it has itself been informed.

We all speak for ourselves, of course. For me, in recent years, thinking about and teaching 'English' has often had to be against the grain of official prescription and public pronouncement. This is not a matter of choice but of conviction. The heart of this conviction is that 'English' cannot *be* 'English' unless it is rooted in and unified by the study of literature. Therein lies its claim to be a distinctive curriculum subject. Recent public accounts of 'English' (see chapter 4) have shown the imprint of this conception but faintly. To invoke the standards to be found in literature itself (what Ezra Pound described as 'language charged with meaning to the utmost possible degree') is frequently to find the public language wanting: uninspired and uninspiring. If, for instance, the language in which the Office for Standards in Education (OFSTED) reports on the teaching of 'English' can be so described (as I suggest in chapter 1), it is because OFSTED does no more than avail itself of the public currency of discussion put into circulation by the first National Curriculum Order for English.

That currency was not of course fresh minted in 1990. It owed its shape and values partly to forces we can identify in the language and culture of the 1980s more generally (chapter 2) and partly to the unsettled state of professional opinion amongst teachers of English. The 'consensus' 'English' that the Cox Committee (1989) claimed to have articulated (it was the basis of the 1990 Order) reflected the decline of that unifying conviction which a much earlier committee (Newbolt, 1921) had argued was the only possible basis for the subject: that the study of the English language and the study of its literature are 'inextricably connected'. This integral view of literacy, which is still active in the best English teaching (see chapter 5), left little mark on the Cox Report. Literature being one way in which 'messages are conveyed', the energies of the committee spent themselves in a marathon of definition which left 'English' with vast responsibilities and no centre.

The lapse of that unifying conviction has thus had serious consequences. It seems to me that at the present time we need a renewed sense of its provenance and formative powers. In chapter 3, therefore, I sketch its cultural roots and influence and in both chapters 3 and 4 some of the symptoms of its decline. It is a decline that has led to the kind of anomaly examined in chapters 5 and 6: the formulaic assessment of both the written and the spoken word is, I suggest, out of touch with the proper standards we should apply to both (an anomaly which the revised Order of 1995 will not correct).

The sense of where we should be looking for those standards has been weakened from the outset by the very structure of National Curriculum English. Had Speaking and Listening not been split off and assessed separately from Reading and from Writing (in my view a mistaken decision that has distorted the purposes of English teaching and been disproportionately expensive of teachers' energies) we might be better placed to achieve the integrated *understanding* of the subject upon which the 'integrated programme' called for in the 1995 Order needs to be based. The consequences of not integrating our thinking about speaking and listening with our feeling for literature and its history are dealt with in chapters 6 and 7, particularly in relation to the bitter controversy over the teaching and assessment of spoken standard English. *Force majeure* has now moved the study of literature nearer to the centre of 'English'. That at least provides the occasion for re-thinking the special contribution English teachers might make to the development of the spoken word. Our conclusions, I suggest, will not make it easy to defend the present splintered structure of National Curriculum English.

CHAPTER ONE
The Public Language of 'English'

> ...accustom yourself to reflect on the words you use, hear or read, their birth, derivation and history. For if words are not THINGS, they are LIVING POWERS, by which the things of most importance to mankind are actuated, combined and humanized.
>
> (Coleridge, Preface to *Aids to Reflection*)

'What English is on the curriculum *for* is not really explored here with any rigour'. So said a dissenting member of Sir John Kingman's Committee of Inquiry into the Teaching of English Language (DES, 1988). Seven years on, with the experiment of the first National Curriculum Order for English at an end and the second in prospect, it would seem reasonable to expect that question to have been more or less settled. However, anyone expecting the answer to be reflected in OFSTED's *English: a review of inspection findings 1993/94* (1995) would have been disappointed. OFSTED reports on 'performance' in English; nowhere does it consider questions of purpose. It performs a monitoring function only, working purely within the terms and categories of the National Curriculum. Helpfully, however, (if unintentionally) the review thus focuses a question that the inception of the revised National Curriculum Order for English (1995) makes particularly acute.

The incoming Order, like its predecessor, is 'English' in its public form. For most people outside the teaching profession (and, probably, for many within it) this *is* 'English'. That cannot and should not be the case for teachers of the subject. In practice, English teachers have variously adhered to, accommodated, or in part eluded the National Curriculum. Total conformity could hardly be expected in a section of the profession whose traditions have typically stressed the scope allowed for the teacher's own creative energies and cultured judgement. Traditionally there has often been a healthy tension between the individualism invited by the subject and the systems within which it was obliged to work. Until the coming of the National Curriculum it was possible for many teachers of 'English' to reconcile the two: to teach the subject according to their best conscience *and* to ensure that their pupils were not thereby disabled when it came to public certification of their achievements.

National Curriculum English abruptly curtailed this traditional freedom, compelling teachers to work within a structure and to assess their pupils according to detailed criteria with which they might profoundly disagree. One of the troubling consequences of the centralizing of the curriculum is that it is increasingly difficult to hold on to (indeed to remember) the traditions it displaced. Authority regularly appeals to teachers' 'professional judgement'; not usually, however, so that it shall exercise itself in the independent and disinterested way that belongs to all judgement but in order to 'deliver the National Curriculum' or to 'make it work'. 'Professional judgement' is free only to decide on the means whereby 'the requirements of the National Curriculum' might be fulfilled. The challenge at the present time is to maintain the integrity of 'professional judgement' against the rhetoric that would make it the servant of a system it must be free to question.

To do so is becoming increasingly difficult, for the 'public language' of English is monopolized by the terms and categories of the National Curriculum. OFSTED's review reflects and, by virtue of its official standing, confirms and propagates that public language. For that language to be healthy, for it to be felt worthy of the *standards* we are asked to see OFSTED as protecting, teachers need to be persuaded that it speaks for them, that it connects with their beliefs and practices. Will they recognize themselves and be reassured when they are told that

> An essential ingredient of high quality teaching at these stages [Key Stages 3 and 4] is the teacher's confident knowledge about language, understanding of the concept of literary genres, and acquaintance with a broad range of literary and non-fiction texts.
>
> (OFSTED, 1995)

This contrives to be blunt, bland and contradictory. Despite the authoritative tone this is not a disciplined use of language. Can mere 'acquaintance' be enough in the case of literature when the more substantial 'knowledge' is necessary with 'language'? Can the understanding of a 'concept' be as 'essential' as either? More seriously, 'knowledge about language' (a substantial and contentious component of the outgoing Order) is not even a shadow of itself in the new Order. How can standards be maintained by the virtual elimination of such an 'essential ingredient'? OFSTED is not troubled by this fundamental question for one simple reason: its review is conducted entirely within the terms and categories of the outgoing National Curriculum Order. Moreover its conception of 'high quality teaching' is entirely constrained by those terms: 'good teaching is based on National Curriculum requirements'. From which it follows (nonsensically) that when the 'requirements' change, the nature of good teaching changes too: it is redefined in conformity with whatever official version of English prevails (OFSTED avoids drawing attention to this bizarre logic by nowhere mentioning that its report is published as the old Order expires and its replacement comes into view). 'Good teaching' of course is essentially personal. The 'essential ingredient' is a compound of intellectual, moral and emotional elements that are in practice inseparable. OFSTED's adjurations to teachers (the tone is somewhat impatient, frequently severe and admonitory) evoke a quite different conception. Amongst the 'key issues' identified are the following (my italics): 'Secondary schools should:

- take *early and vigorous action to identify and remedy serious weaknesses* in pupils' writing.

All schools should:

- ensure that all pupils *develop technical and organisational skills* in writing systematically.
- take *all possible steps to bring about a rapid improvement in the performance* of boys within English.'

'Professional judgement' is likely to retort that neither good writing nor indeed 'boys' (that ungraspable, undifferentiated category) can be as readily brought on as OFSTED's muscular vocabulary suggests. What are teachers to do with exhortations pitched at this level of generality and in terms so questionable? OFSTED's tone is not an invitation to debate or reflection. Its business-like briskness assumes that the essential questions are long settled – questions that in teachers' daily practice are as inescapable as they are awkward: *how* is 'weakness' in writing to be converted into strength? What is the relationship between 'technical and organisational skills' and good writing? The inspectorial briskness seems to rest on no surer grasp of the nature and purposes of 'English' than is supplied by the ready-made phrases of the National Curriculum. 'Good standards...are marked by effective writing for different purposes, a developing sense of the usefulness of drafting and growing skills of sentence construction and vocabulary'. OFSTED's conception of writing seems to be almost entirely technical, embracing even those aspects of the command of language to which it is demonstrably irrelevant – what can it mean to speak of vocabulary as a 'skill'?

The physically strenuous metaphors upon which OFSTED's exhortations depend belong to a rhetoric with which official publications have made us very familiar in the last ten years or so. In this rhetoric the teacher tends to be cast as a technician with a system to maintain. The imputation of technical duties neglected (notwithstanding that 'the quality of teaching is satisfactory or better in 80% of lessons across all stages') is unmistakable. After all, if the problems identified can be resolved – and 'rapid improvements' brought about – by early, systematic, vigorous action and 'active intervention', then such problems should never have arisen in the first place. The image of the teacher evoked in OFSTED's formulation of key issues is that of troubleshooter and action-man: his own 'performance' is to be judged by his knowledge of the system and his willingness to submit to it. There are 'National Curriculum requirements' and there's an end of it. This is a rhetoric that depends for its effect on the belief that improvements lie in the more efficient operation of systems ('systematically' rivals 'skills' as a watchword in OFSTED's review) rather than in the creativity of individuals.

'The more flaccid and abstract the language of politics becomes', said the Italian novelist Italo Calvino, 'the more we are conscious of a tacit demand for a different language, more direct and personal. More provocative too' (Calvino, 1987). To read OFSTED's review is keenly to feel such a 'demand'. OFSTED's subservience to the established official vocabularies and the assumptions they express means that, as a contribution to a national debate on what are indisputably matters of national importance, the review is null. Its value, perhaps, is that it exhibits in a peculiarly concentrated way the poverty of a 'public' language which has become detached from the culture and the history of the subject. (The earliest forms of the SATs produced a similar sense of dislocation: they were disconnected from the best contemporary practice and vitiated by the worst practice of the past (SEAC, 1993).)

Constrained by the obsolescent formulas of the 1990 Order, silent on the implications of its replacement, OFSTED's language as emphatically excludes the past as it does the future. That there is a history to the discussion of those 'key issues' is neither mentioned nor implied. Whether addressed to the teaching profession or considered as a stimulus to public debate, OFSTED's language thus lacks generative power: the test of the value and effectiveness of a public language. History indeed supplies the instructive contrast: in the Newbolt Report, *The Teaching of English in England,* of 1921. For Newbolt, language is embodied history as well as an instrument for present use. To the extent that 'English' survives with any coherence, it is still indebted to a nineteenth-century conception of language, literature and sensibility that came to be voiced in Newbolt's assertion of the

> incontrovertible primary fact, that for English children no form of knowledge can take precedence of a knowledge of English, no form of

literature can take precedence of English literature: and that the two are so inextricably connected as to form the only basis possible for a national education.

(HMSO, 1921, p.14)

The tones are again authoritative, passionate even. What distinguishes this from OFSTED, however, is that it prompts and repays contemplation on its own terms. It provokes us, indeed, to attend to that essential question of what 'English is on the curriculum *for*': what can it mean to speak of those two 'forms of knowledge' (neither of them synonymous with 'knowledge about language') as 'inextricably connected'? What is it about them that justifies the implication of shared being, the *only* basis possible for a national education? Does the claim still stand if we substitute the word 'curriculum' for 'education'? What are the 'forms of knowledge' peculiar to English as a curriculum subject? Do these forms imply the need for a different kind of attention to language from that demanded in teachers of other subjects? The emphatic return of English literature in the revised Order makes this an opportune (though it is always a necessary) question. If a 'knowledge of English' and a 'knowledge of English literature' are inextricable, why does the revised Order retain the tripartite structure of its predecessor: Speaking and Listening; Reading; Writing? Is it sensible to extricate the elements of English in this way and then to insist that teachers fuse them in 'an integrated programme'?

'Education', said Cicero, 'frees us from the constraints of the present'. OFSTED's language locks its readers into the present, denying perspectives that might challenge the philosophies it serves. The articulation of such perspectives is the basis of a liberal education. To believe as much nowadays puts schoolteachers and teacher-educators in an invidious position. Teacher-educators (I speak as one here) tend to feel themselves trapped between contradictory obligations: between, on the one hand, the pragmatic obligation to prepare the next generation of teachers to implement National Curriculum 'requirements' and, on the other, their established, overriding duty to call those 'requirements' into critical question. In practice this means trying never to lose sight of that important question of 'what English is on the curriculum *for*'. It means working towards an articulate understanding of the 'forms of knowledge' that define or should define the subject. Teacher-educators and schoolteachers too are morally in the position of the literary critic as D.H. Lawrence saw it: 'a good critic should give his reader a few standards to go by' (Lawrence, 1961). Wherever those standards come from, they cannot be supplied by the changing 'requirements of the National Curriculum'. Indeed, those 'requirements' make it more than ever necessary that we should pay attention to that 'different language, more direct and personal', wherever we find it. As the curriculum becomes more centralized and the official language of the subject more entrenched, it is vital to maintain the sense of an alternative – 'professional judgement' is nothing unless it is also confidently individual judgement. Illumination and provocation will come from various and sometimes unexpected quarters – and not always from 'English'. In my own case little has recently concentrated my thoughts about writing more powerfully than the work of the Italian chemist and survivor of Auschwitz, Primo Levi. In thinking about the spoken word, as about standard English and dialect, it has been Tony Harrison's poetry and Toni Morrison's novel *Jazz* that have been most 'provocative' (to read *Jazz* is to feel what it can mean to speak of *a people* as it comes to know and celebrate itself through the rhythms of a spoken language that are also the rhythms of a musical culture). In recent years I have gained a more urgent sense of the importance of literature through reading Nadezdha Mandelstam, Joseph Brodsky and Vaclav Havel (each of whom 'learned that words still count for something when you can go to prison for them' (Havel, 1991)) than from most critics writing in English, Ted Hughes and Seamus Heaney excepted. As for writing about English teaching itself nothing for me has equalled Jill Pirrie's *On Common Ground* (1987) and *Apple Fire* (1993), both classic statements of 'what English is on the curriculum *for*'.

All teachers of English need the opportunity to listen to voices of this quality. The strongest criticism to be made of the first National Curriculum Order for English was that its complexities allowed teachers so little space to do this: to read, reflect, experiment and, in the unsystematic way of such activities, to strengthen their hold on the purposes of English (which cannot be simply stated or deduced from any curriculum document) and to maintain that sense of an alternative. Historical perspective is indispensable here. Children, says the new Order, are 'to consider the [historical] development of English'. So must we, not in the technical ways prescribed for children but qualitatively. OFSTED's parched prose (prose of the present tense) cannot be explained entirely as a sign of political intervention. The history that bears upon the writing includes changing ideas about the nature of language and the responsibilities of English teachers; it includes the steady dissolution of those convictions that inspired the Newbolt Committee to write of the subject with manifest pride and idealistic hope (Newbolt would have found it incomprehensible that no more should be asked of teachers than – pallid phrase – an 'acquaintance' with literary texts). English has undeniably suffered from insensitive political intrusion in the last few years and OFSTED's tone reflects its influence; but the decline of convictions about the purposes of English cannot be so simply explained. We need to understand the origins, nature and influence of those convictions and the part the English teaching profession itself has played in their decline (chapter 3 explores this): a decline that in recent years has, in my view, made the profession more vulnerable to the grosser forms of political pressure than it should have been. As the forms of political *centralism* began to re-shape English in the eighties, what we needed to hear, loud and clear, was the note of *centrality*. What too often we heard instead was the note of intellectual parochialism: from the A level examiner rejecting the 'reverential notion of literature as "the best English"' because it 'renders English open to the charge of being a snob subject' (Jones and West, 1988); from academics who could speak of the literature of the past as 'now largely inert literary texts' (Beynon *et al.*, 1983); from the Cox Report (DES, 1989), reducing 'the heritage of literature' to one way in which 'messages are conveyed'. Eventually, therefore, the ill-conceived and short-lived Key Stage 3 anthology (DFE, 1993a) was summarily imposed upon a profession supposedly neglectful of its own traditions; 'canonical' authors have been inserted into the 1995 Order for the same reasons. Few teachers wanted either.

Ironically, however, since teachers now have no choice but to give those authors very close attention, the texts themselves may help us to recover an adequate language in which to think about 'English'. For any teacher persuaded (as I am) that literature should be 'at the heart of the English curriculum' (DES, 1986), literature will be an authentic source of standards in the teaching of English: standards in the language we observe, use and attempt to develop in the young. We all have our favourite demonstrations, touchstones that have helped us to settle our beliefs about the 'forms of knowledge' we are concerned with as English teachers. Amongst my own demonstrations, ever more firmly inextricable from my sense of 'what English is on the curriculum *for*', are Wordsworth's 'One Summer evening...' (from *The Prelude*); Blake's short lyric 'The Sick Rose' and D.J. Enright's poem 'A Polished Performance'. *There* is that 'different language, more direct and personal', language at its least 'flaccid and abstract', English to think about 'English' with. An intense, contemplative focus on texts such as these (the possible range of examples is of course immense) can illuminate the purposes of English teaching with a generative power that no curriculum document (however detailed its tabulations of 'objectives' and 'skills') will ever possess. The results can be uncomfortable. At a time when the public rhetoric does indeed elide 'English' and the 'requirements of the National Curriculum' it is more than ever necessary (as I tell my students) to retain a calm and strongly-founded independence. To open oneself to the 'living powers' at work in those texts (as my students are invited to do at various points in their PGCE course) is to deepen one's sense of the 'forms of knowledge' which they draw upon and extend. I choose passages of this kind and quality because they enable us to explore Newbolt's memorable contention that 'English is not merely the medium of our thought, it is the very stuff and process of it. It is itself the English mind in which we live and work' (HMSO, 1921).

What does it mean for us now to speak thus of the native language as an inward possession? These poems supply a kind of answer. Theirs is a language for thinking about 'English': for subjecting the terms and categories of National Curriculum English to the most logical of tests: by the standards of the best English available to us. Implicitly this is recognized in the Order itself to be literature: Wordsworth and Blake, for instance, are 'major poets' within the prescribed range of authors for Key Stages 3 and 4. They supply us with powerful support in considering the always fundamental question for 'English': the question of value (which is another way of saying, 'what is "English" on the curriculum *for*?'). In considering language used with the scruple and intensity to be found in those authors do we find the prescriptive language of the National Curriculum to have the 'generative power' I said was lacking in OFSTED's: the power to generate coherent practice in the light of articulate principle? Do we feel the pressure of such principle, for instance, behind the 'requirement' that children 'should be taught' 'the main characteristics that distinguish literature of high quality'; or that they 'should be taught to extract meaning beyond the literal' and 'analyse and discuss hidden meanings' and, in their own writing, to 'develop their use of poetic devices'? The question of value is also a question of choice: of what goes into school English and what doesn't. As in these passages we ponder language 'charged with meaning to the utmost degree' (Ezra Pound) are we content that time not given to such language is instead well-spent on investigating 'the differences between speech and writing' or 'the vocabulary of standard English and dialectal variations'? My contention is that an openness to the example of such language is unlikely to leave us sanguine about the quality of the 'official' language. An encounter with real precision in language will leave us dissatisfied with its show: the 1995 Order requires that pupils should be taught 'the characteristics of different kinds of writing e.g. argument, commentary, narrative, dialogue' (DFE, 1995). These characteristics (like 'the characteristics that distinguish literature of high quality') have about them the air of what Wordsworth called

> that false secondary power
> By which we multiply distinctions, then
> Deem that our puny boundaries are things
> That we perceive and not that we have made.
>
> (Wordsworth, 1971, p.85)

We learn about writing *from* writing. Viewed in the light of Wordsworth's celebrated account of his escapade with the stolen boat on Ullswater, the tabulation of the 'variety of purposes' for writing at Key Stages 3 and 4 begins to look like the invention of those 'puny boundaries':

> One summer evening (led by her) I found
> A little boat tied to a willow tree
> Within a rocky cave, its usual home.
> Straight I unloosed her chain, and stepping in
> Pushed from the shore. It was an act of stealth
> And troubled pleasure, nor without the voice
> Of mountain-echoes did my boat move on;
> Leaving behind her still, on either side,
> Small circles glittering idly in the moon,
> Until they melted all into one track
> Of sparkling light. But now, like one who rows,
> Proud of his skill, to reach a chosen point
> With an unswerving line, I fixed my view
> Upon the summit of a craggy ridge,
> The horizon's utmost boundary, for above
> Was nothing but the stars and the grey sky.
> She was an elfin pinnace; lustily
> I dipped my oars into the silent lake,
> And, as I rose upon the stroke, my boat
> Went heaving through the water like a swan;
> When, from behind that craggy steep till then
> The horizon's bound, a huge peak, black and huge,
> As if with voluntary power instinct
> Upreared its head. I struck and struck again,
> And growing still in stature the grim shape
> Towered up between me and the stars, and still,
> For so it seemed, with purpose of its own
> And measured motion like a living thing,
> Strode after me. With trembling oars I turned,
> And through the silent water stole my way
> Back to the covert of the willow tree;
> There in her mooring-place I left my bark, –
> And through the meadows homeward went, in grave
> And serious mood; but after I had seen

That spectacle, for many days, my brain
Worked with a dim and undetermined sense
Of unknown modes of being; o'er my thoughts
There hung a darkness, call it solitude
Or blank desertion. No familiar shapes
Remained, no pleasant images of trees,
Of sea or sky, no colours of green fields;
But huge and mighty forms, that do not live
Like living men, moved slowly through the mind
By day, and were a trouble to my dreams.

(Wordsworth, 1971, pp. 55 and 57)

Is Wordsworth here writing for 'aesthetic and imaginative purposes'; or 'to inform others through instruction, explanation, argument, narrative, reportage, description, persuasion'; or 'to develop thinking through review, analysis, hypothesis and summary' (DFE, 1995)? The implication of so comprehensive a list is that we should have no trouble in 'matching' Wordsworth to one of those purposes and in identifying the 'particular skills' he used in realizing it. Writing, said the 1990 Order, reflected the 'ability to construct and convey meaning in written language matching style to audience and purpose' (DES, 1990). No such matching is possible. The proposition is unreal. *All* of those 'purposes' are encompassed within that one passage. We can say the same of most good novels too, from Dickens to Rushdie. Indeed, it is the inclusiveness of so much of the best writing, of the very stuff of 'English', that gives it its power, both as an example and an inspiration. What it means to accept that inclusiveness as a principle shaping the teaching of writing I shall discuss in chapter 5. That it was a principle shaping Wordsworth's own is obvious. He would have scorned the suggestion that in giving an account of the 'growth of a poet's mind' in *The Prelude* his purposes were 'aesthetic and imaginative': a phrase which, in perpetuating an unreal distinction between thought and feeling, confirms the commonplace misconception of literature as cut off from those 'real or realistic purposes' to which the curricular documents preceding the 1990 Order gave such exaggerated attention. Wordsworth defies such categories and distinctions. The 'living powers' in his words give us entry to an intense spiritual drama: physical, psychological, emotional, moral. No one term is adequate to describe the experience. As we are led through the various stages of the drama we are conscious, as Wordsworth himself so clearly was, of the boundaries of inner and outer worlds merging: this is a physical experience of grave psychological import; or is it, rather, an inner turmoil achieving outward display (its 'objective correlative')? It is both. The scene lives in the poet's intense imagining, from which it only *seems* that we can detach it. For there is no scene, no physical reality, save in the imagination that recalls and relives it.

'Drama', 'physical': we need to hear the speaking voice as we read such poetry. Wordsworth, one remembers, often composed aloud whilst walking. To voice the words, to read them aloud, is to open oneself more fully to their meanings. For teachers of English there is no more important method; for pupils no form of 'oral work' more clearly native to the subject. ('Reading aloud' is altogether ignored in the Speaking and Listening requirements for Key Stages 3 and 4.) 'Certain authors', says the Canadian critic Roger Shattuck, in an essay of seminal importance in the teaching of literature and the spoken word, 'cry out for oral performance' (Shattuck, 1984). Amongst writers in English he instances Whitman, Emily Dickinson, T.S. Eliot and Wordsworth. What will the recreating voice need to be alive to in the passage quoted? To explore this question is to find one way into the 'heart of English'; to *feel* what it means for literature to 'extend...moral and emotional understanding' (DFE, 1995).

The opening four and a half lines call for no dramatic emphasis; the scene is set in a straightforward, literal fashion. But then, abruptly, come the phrases that register the nature of the act to be described: 'it was an act of stealth and troubled pleasure'; the soft sounds convey the feeling of stepping beyond bounds and qualify the tranquillity evoked in the lines that follow. Already the guilty consciousness is present in 'the voice of the mountain echoes', the voice of what will soon be all but a 'living thing'. 'But now,...': there is a sustained moment of triumphant pride – and the phrase needs to be sounded with the kind of single-minded determination fitting the skilled oarsman thrilled by his own powers, sustained by and in unison with the waters apparently under his control. The muscularity is precisely rendered; the lines are charged with the energy of pride upon its pinnacle:

> And, as I rose upon the stroke, my boat
> Went heaving through the water like a swan;

What follows, in its rhythmic control, its deliberate repetitions, its alternation of abstractions and urgent, physically apt monosyllables, is the magnificently charged central moment of this drama. The force of the monosyllables 'huge' and 'struck', their repetition urgently evoking the tranced terror of the moment, is to convert abstraction into its opposite: 'voluntary power' and 'measured motion' are assimilated to the general and overwhelming sense of a being set upon overcoming the spirit only recently so proud. The placing of 'upreared' and 'strode', the steady ineluctable rhythms of that final sentence, make their wonderfully judged contribution. This indeed is 'emotion recollected in tranquillity'. However, like Wordsworth himself, we don't find ourselves giving it a name. In him it induces a 'grave and serious mood'; what has induced that mood has been made a 'living thing' in the measure of his line. But now it is over, this central, overwhelming moment, and a kind of calm returns to the verse. However, though the young oarsman 'stole' his way 'back to the covert of the willow tree', this is no ordinary tale of guilty conscience, no simple moral tale. If morality is mixed in with the consequences of this proud act its scene of operation is larger and more mysterious than normal. The oppression that hangs over him is beyond accounting for in everyday terms of cause and effect. Indeed we perhaps need to speak of depression rather than oppression. For the consequence is a kind of alienation from the familiar world – 'no pleasant images of trees/Of sea or sky, no colours of green fields'. The 'grave and serious mood' is evoked in lines that stand in conspicuous contrast to the dynamic, physically taut rhythms that accompanied the moment of mastery. Now there comes a different mystery that can only be evoked through negation: 'a dim and undetermined sense/Of unknown modes of being...blank desertion'. This blankness is penetrated only by the residues of the forces that induced it: they live troublingly again in the last three lines. 'Troubled pleasure' has led to 'troubled dreams'.

What Wordsworth recollects in this passage is an episode in the boy's 'moral education'. But the standard phrase won't do. It excludes the mystery, the mixed sense of pain and privilege that such an advance in consciousness entails. There is no scheme of values, no ideology implied in such an advance; it is a growth of spiritual awareness, of the power to know something of one's inevitable but permanently inscrutable relation to the universe into which one has been born. It must have been passages of such undeniable power that 'saved' J.S. Mill (Mill, 1873). His emotional and spiritual starvation was due to an education and an upbringing based on the illusion that a sense of our place and duty in the world can be deduced from the ways of this world alone. Wordsworth's best poetry irresistibly demolishes that illusion, opens up the way (it certainly did for Mill) for currents of feeling that can find no justification in a purely material, utilitarian world. To read this passage faithfully, to give true voice to the various stages of the drama, is to enact a phase of spiritual growth; it is to work with the resources of the material world – resources most skilfully and beautifully ordered – so as to demonstrate their limits. In savouring the words and the rhythms we sense more vividly than we can by the eye alone the heightened intensity of perception they make possible. We are, incidentally, learning about language in the most positive way, a way that engages our humanity at a depth beyond the reach of the abstract 'knowledge about language' from which so much has been expected in recent years.

In the case of Blake's 'The Sick Rose' we are conscious not so much of an extension of our perceptions as of the deepening and intensifying of those we already possess. Some words seem more deeply rooted than others in the English language, to branch more widely than others within that complex of phrase and idiom that keeps a language alive. There can be few speakers of English for whom the word 'rose' will not have such roots. You do not need to know the detailed wealth of symbolism, the heraldic richness and the prolific incidence of rose imagery in English poetry to be touched by its centrality in English cultural history. It is one of those words whose significances have penetrated every aspect of English life (indeed of European culture); to speak the language is almost certainly to be in touch at some level, whether it be of high or popular art, of religion or civic display, with those significances. Blake's 'The Sick Rose' is in touch with the traditional resonances of the word at a variety of levels, the perfect illustration of an art both sophisticated and popular, endlessly creative of fresh meaning but indissociable from its preliterate history. Blake is in touch with the history of our sensibilities as speakers of English, with the common spoken language that we hear in the oral tradition upon which he draws:

> O Rose, thou art sick!
> The invisible worm
> That flies in the night,
> In the howling storm,
>
> Has found out thy bed
> Of crimson joy:
> And his dark secret love
> Does thy life destroy.

(Blake, 1972, p.213)

The poem draws on and confirms a common possession of meanings. Ask a group of fifteen year olds who have yet to read the poem what they associate with the word 'rose' and you will get a predictably narrow but telling range of responses: thorn, scented, decay, love, romantic, blood, passion – all of which are obviously enough contained in Blake's poem, part of a common stock. The fascination of the poem is the rich play it makes with that stock, the vast field of possible meaning it opens out from within its tiny compass. No two readers will experience the poem in the same way even though it is founded upon so readily provable a common possession. 'The Sick Rose' is the perfect example of the most celebrated of the 'Auguries of Innocence':

14

To see a World in a Grain of Sand
And a Heaven in a Wild Flower,
Hold Infinity in the palm of your hand,
And Eternity in an hour.

(Blake, 1972, p.431)

That the depthless symbolism of the rose *is* a common possession has important implications for teachers and learners. Here is that inextricable connectedness of which Newbolt speaks; here is the 'form of knowledge' that belongs distinctively to 'English'. To demonstrate in that straightforward way that Blake draws on an existing sensibility in native speakers of the English language is to narrow the distance between art and its audience. It is to show that common words and simple means may serve complex ends. This, one wants to say, is 'basic English'; night, storm, bed, joy, love. To be brought up in the English language is, in Keats' phrase, to know these words 'on our pulses', to possess them at such a depth as to make them synonymous with our being. They are words for which no dictionary definition can possibly suffice; their resonances, their ramifications, their potentialities are a matter of our life-experience. They are great communal words but at the same time they are for any of us deeply coloured by our individual, unique experience. That is why, after we have explored the associations of rose, storm, night, bed, love, when we have agreed that the myth of the serpent in Eden is central to the act of destruction, that the love which is dark and secret is a love so compromised as to unhinge the word itself from its Christian meaning – that is why the poem remains inexhaustible: not as a richly symbolic picture of an event or an experience that is past but as an image of what is and what may always be. It is one of those poems of which it may be truly said that it cannot be the same for us at sixteen as it is at forty. The reach and potency of the words will not be the same; they will change as we change and are changed. There is a kind of assurance to be drawn from this continuity, what earlier writers wouldn't have stinted to call 'solace'. For, whilst 'The Sick Rose' is by no means a comfortable or comforting vision, it has the solid standing of a myth that will stand the test of time, whatever transformations it undergoes in our individual experience. This is English as 'the very stuff and process of our thought', a truly inward possession. Such an understanding is still the inspiration for some richly productive English teaching (see chapter 5) but, for reasons I explore in chapter 3, it is nowadays neither as widespread nor as formative as it once was.

Blake works with the grain of the language, so that our common feeling is of being taken forward with an imagination that has begun its journey from a common point, a foundation on which native speakers of English are united. (How else can we come to share and accept the truth of a vision that is the more vivid for being inexplicit?) If D.J. Enright starts from that same foundation it is a much shakier thing than it was for either Wordsworth or Blake. It is the treachery rather than the trustworthiness of words that occupies this quintessentially modern writer:

> A Polished Performance
>
> Citizens of the polished capital
>   Sigh for the towns up country,
> And their innocent simplicity.
>
> People in the towns up country
>   Applaud the unpolished innocence
> Of the distant villages.
>
> Dwellers in the distant villages
>   Speak of a simple unspoilt girl,
> Living alone, deep in the bush.
>
> Deep in the bush we found her,
>   Large and innocent of eye,
> Among gentle gibbons and mountain ferns.
>
> Perfect for the part, perfect,
>   Except for the dropsy
> Which comes from polished rice.
>
> In the capital our film is much admired,
>   Its gentle gibbons and mountain ferns,
> Unspoilt, unpolished, large and innocent of eye.
>
> (Enright, 1981, p.32)

This is a poem to be enjoyed in one way as *play*, not simply in the most obvious sense of a play on and with the key words, but as the writer's inventive, delighted and ironic manipulation of the stereotypes that make it all too likely that we will at one time or another have been amongst those citizens of the 'polished capital' admiring that factitious film. He is canny enough to include himself in the general indictment: inevitably we come to see the poem itself as a 'polished performance'. The guilt, he would seem to say, that should arise in the comfortable cosmopolitan mind as it contemplates a by now transparently dishonest film may also belong in the mind that crafts the poem: art may be the escape route from the very realities it discloses; the inescapable ironies arising from the repetition of 'polished' and 'innocent' may be savoured by the reader at the expense of the indictment they express.

'A Polished Performance' is, in my experience, an extraordinarily fertile poem, whether as a focus for 'language work' in school or for the discussion of 'what English is on the curriculum *for*' with PGCE students. We cannot of course consider the language apart from the personal, social and political implications to which the poem directs us. What are those implications? Our stereotypes of 'the third world' and our ignorance of the facts that might correct them; the habitual and indulgent selectiveness of the images made for our entertainment; our proneness to versions of sentimental pastoralism: all these certainly. But to abstract them in this way is to risk betraying the texture of the work from which they arise; and it is to the texture of the work that we are primarily committed. How truthful are the ironies of Enright's poem? When we consult our own experience, our own considered view of the world and our uses of language, how troubling or diverting do we find his play with words and the criticism they express? We shall find ourselves discussing the chameleon character of the key words as the changes of meaning to which they are subject are revealed through the writer's skill. We shall accordingly see how our own uses of such words are frequently loose and ill-considered – that *we* are capable of falling into the clichés of expression and behaviour so beautifully and discomfortingly caught up in the final, resonant line of the poem, a line that gathers up the varying connotations of the four epithets as they have previously been evoked and invites us to reflect on the changes wrought in our own view by what the poet has done with them.

To contemplate poems so different from each other as those three is to gain a deepened sense of the range of the English language, of the variety of ways in which it has been and is being used to illuminate both inner and outer worlds. For all their differences, what unites them is a scrupulousness with words, an instinctive determination in their authors to make them count in our intellectual and emotional lives, to 'charge' words with meaning. To contemplate language used in this way and to do so habitually is to strengthen our hold on words and absorb the standards by which we come to judge all uses of language, spoken and written. We cannot abstract those standards; we cannot convert them into criteria 'against which' (to use the current telling jargon) we measure the quality of other writers. The contemplation of the exceptional in language (and this should be the principal activity of English teaching at all academic levels) ought, under the guidance of a sympathetic teacher, to produce an attitude towards language that itself makes for 'higher standards'.[1] That attitude will entail a respect for words based on an experienced

---

[1]Obviously these are not standards of the kind measured by SATs or GCSE results; they are not what the National Commission on Education means when it says that 'Reading standards among 10/11 and 15/16 year olds have changed little since 1945' (Brooks *et al.*, 1995). Such statements tell us little about what really matters: improvement or decline in the quality of attention to language. There is no guarantee that public examinations will promote one rather than the other.

recognition of their powers; it will thus lead to a disciplined vigilance in the uses to which we put them and a comparable vigilance in the face of those to which we are exposed. In short, the attitude will be a critical attitude.

Properly interpreted, it is to such an attitude that Newbolt's conception of the two 'inextricable' 'forms of knowledge' leads. To have gone deeply into those poems is to have moved towards an answer to that essential question: 'what is English on the curriculum *for*?' To understand what can be done with words at the level of those demonstrations is to deepen one's sense of what *they* are for. Language used with such scruple and intensity is not of course the constant fare of 'English'; it is nonetheless a touchstone for deciding what that fare should comprise. Those words compel attention to the experience they embody. What we seek above all in 'English' is to develop useful habits of attention to language and we will only do that if we teach it through language of a quality that compels attention. Much centralized curricular directive has discouraged the development of these habits and the public language of 'English' itself exhibits the decline.

Inwardness with such language will not in itself guarantee the 'high quality teaching' of which OFSTED speaks; such teaching is nonetheless impossible without it. Inwardness, being intangible, is not part of OFSTED's vocabulary or understanding; yet it is (again in its phrase) an 'essential ingredient'. It implies much more than an 'acquaintance with a broad range of literary and non-fiction texts', 'acquaintance' being no substitute for depth of understanding. Inwardness is essential whereas 'knowledge about language' (in the meaning the phrase had in the 1990 Order) and 'understanding of the concept of literary genres' is not. This note of abstraction is the characteristic note of 'official' English: a teacher who recognizes stories, poems, novels and essays when she sees them doesn't need to worry about the *concept* of genres. Neither should she have to worry about teaching her pupils to 'recognize, analyse and evaluate the characteristic features of different types of text in print and other media' (DFE, 1995). And being essential, inwardness is useful. For teachers of 'English' it constitutes a form of discipline which will impose itself in the making of judgements on matters large and small: OFSTED and National Curriculum documents on the one hand and day-by-day choices of classroom content and method on the other. It helps us to see, for instance, what is wrong with the 'requirement' that children be 'taught the main characteristics of literary language' and the 'characteristics that distinguish literature of high quality'. How far would such teaching take students in understanding writing of the quality I have been discussing here? Despite the show of exactitude, of precise classification and distinction, those are empty phrases more likely to distort than promote good practice. Language of the quality demonstrated in my examples has in recent years not been allowed its proper place in our thinking about English. In so far as the public language for the discussion of English has been deficient, it is in large measure because it has become dislocated from the sources that should have nourished it, principally English literature. The reasons for that dislocation are not to be found in 'English' or indeed in education alone.

CHAPTER TWO
Words in the Eighties

> Only when a word has become necessary to him can a man use it safely: if
> he try to impress words by force on a sudden occasion, they will either
> perish of his violence or betray him. No man can decree the value of one
> word, unless it is his own invention; the value which it will have in his hands
> has been decreed by his own past, by the past of his race...unless a man write
> with his whole nature concentrated upon his subject he is unlikely to take
> hold of another man.
>
> (Edward Thomas, 1913, pp.215–216)

In his essay 'Myth and Education' Ted Hughes speaks of the 'rising
prestige of scientific awareness and the lowering prestige of religious
awareness' in our own time; of the impact of 'the scientific ideal' on our
sense of 'the inner world of the body'. 'The first thing we have to
confess', says Hughes, 'is that it [the inner world] cannot be seen
objectively...We solve the problem by never looking inward. We identify
ourselves and all that is wakeful and intelligent with our objective eye,
saying "Let's be objective". That is really no more than saying "Let's be
happy"'. Pressure from the 'scientific ideal' (a 'powerful ideal, it has
created the modern world') has 'persuaded human beings to identify
themselves with what is no more than a narrow mode of perception...We
come to regard the body as no more than a somewhat stupid vehicle...the
exclusiveness of our objective eye, the very strength and brilliance of our
objective intelligence, suddenly turns into stupidity...' (Hughes, 1994).
   Naturally 'objective intelligence' of this kind has a characteristic way
with words. This is what it sounds like:

> Be aware of what turns you on and off, of your own body signals, arousal
> and inhibitions. All this information will make it possible for you to speak
> to a partner from a position of responsibility so that you can both be clear,
> specific and uncritical.

and

> Does your sex life measure up to the sex statistics? If you compare notes

with a friend do you feel you're missing out? Perhaps you're not enjoying sexual encounters any more and feel out of tune with you own body.

(*Cosmopolitan*, February 1985)

These are examples of what the editors of *Cosmopolitan* are inclined to call 'the international language of young women' (*Cosmopolitan*, May 1995). The magazine's readers are offered a new technical language enabling them to talk about their 'needs and anxieties' 'knowledgeably' and 'objectively'; a language for ensuring 'successful communication in sexual situations'. This requires 'self-knowledge'. The word is, as we see above, drastically re-defined; emptied of its established moral and psychological content it becomes a technical concept. This is indeed 'objective intelligence turning into stupidity', the body no more than 'a somewhat stupid vehicle' – the metaphors are of taps and machines. (What, above the most brutal level, could it mean to 'measure' a person's 'sex life' against the 'sex statistics'?) To use words in this way is, in Theodore Roszak's phrases (he is speaking of computers), 'to fall prey to technological idolatry, allowing an invention of our own hands to become the image that dominates our understanding of ourselves and all nature around us' (Roszak, 1986).

Coleridge believed (and very passionately and persuasively demonstrated) that the characteristic language of an age was evidence of 'the direction and main channel in which the thoughts and interests of men were then flowing'. Changes in the uses of words reflected and influenced 'the taste and character, the whole tone of manners and feeling' (White, 1938). In the condition of the language might be tracked 'the current of national tendency'. In the mid-eighties, when I came across the passages quoted, I was reading – and spent some time in school teaching – the poetry of William Blake. I was also getting acquainted with the ground rules for the incoming GCSE, reading the advisory and prescriptive documents as they came out. What struck me was that the language in which the Secondary Examinations Council (SEC) saw fit to address teachers of English had more in common with that of *Cosmopolitan* than either had with the language of Blake. To move from *Cosmopolitan* to the prose of the Council was like moving between adjacent areas of a foreign country. The language – technical, detached and workmanlike – was strikingly similar. The Council's English Working Party was identifying 'subsets of the skills and competencies needed in the subject'. Here the subject was not 'sexual situations' but 'speech situations' and the assessment of 'oral communication'. 'Information' and 'body signals' counted here too. Was this 'the current of national tendency'?

All communication is interactive but it is essential in oral communication to draw particular attention to the relationship between the speaker and the listener. Under the heading Social Context the Working Party has attempted to focus on the interactive nature of the domain. The draft criteria refer not only to specific oral and aural skills but also to paralinguistic features. Great importance is therefore placed both on the manner in which a speaker shows awareness of audience and adapts to it and on the way in which a listener responds to, and thereby furthers, dialogue. Some of the many skills involved are the use of pause or self-correction, the use of intonation, the timing of interventions, the pacing of the utterance, and all the types of non-verbal signals commonly employed in spoken exchanges. These features can be assessed only by on-the-spot observation.

(SEC, 1985)

Now, as a teacher, there was a sense in which I couldn't understand that at all. It resisted sympathetic reading. My eye skated over the unfamiliar words and phrases but they failed to engage my mind; they didn't seem to have anything to do with my experience. When I had been talking with children in classrooms or listening to them talking with one another, I had certainly never thought of myself as taking part in 'oral communication'. Were the new phrases necessary? I didn't know I had 'oral and aural skills' (let alone 'specific' ones). I couldn't imagine what it would mean to be listening, *really* listening, concentrating my whole mind on what was being said – and to be assessing the hapless person talking to me by 'on-the-spot observation'. What exactly was the 'existing expertise' that had so far enabled me to do that in 'real-life situations' (what other kinds of 'situation' were there?). How had a group of adults, sitting down to discuss how they could best help teachers to improve their pupils' spoken English, convinced themselves that this was the way to do it? There was a strong sense of mystification about the novel vocabulary and the scientific tone. What they were describing was something ordinary, human, warm. Their extraordinary vocabulary rendered it inhuman and cold. It seemed to be based on a transparent pretence: that the features of spoken English that we know instinctively to be resistant to scrutiny and adequate description could be objectively measured. Perhaps they could if we really did behave in the way that novel vocabulary suggested, consciously 'using' the 'skills' at our disposal, as aware of our 'body signals' as *Cosmopolitan*'s calculating partners. Were teachers really to be expected to instruct their pupils – *children* – in that kind of calculation? They were. The 'good listener' would 'assist the speaker in pacing his delivery by non-verbal means – nods, frowns etc.' (the dour scientism of this banishes common sense: experienced practitioners of nodding and frowning manage to do it without listening at all). The good speaker would remember to 'use non-verbal signals (eye contact, direction of gaze, posture etc.) to enhance what is said'. Ominously – an invitation to ribaldry this – lower grades were to be reserved for those capable only of 'using a deliberate gesture to support or enhance what is said'.

These very phrases rapidly made their way into the early GCSE syllabuses. They stood for a view of 'English' that places its most significant emphasis upon observable behaviour. There was a profound anomaly here. The English Working Party aimed to identify 'the performance characteristics' expected of candidates at particular grades. A subject which, in its most distinctive traditions, places its emphasis upon the inner, the individual, the imaginative, the symbolic, came to be spoken of as though it were as amenable to assessment as the insides of a combustion engine. To what else, lacking the context, would we expect the phrase 'performance characteristics' to relate? Perhaps only to the kind of performance the *Cosmopolitan* experts are concerned with. There too the inner and the individual are of small account. The *Cosmopolitan* and the SEC writers are united in turning their backs on what is truly significant and distinctive in the experiences with which they are concerned. It is impossible to feel at home in either. They use a language which doesn't tell the truth. It is impossible to persuade oneself in either case that what we are confronted with is the result (in Edward Thomas's words) of someone 'concentrating upon his subject' 'with his whole nature'. Each makes a strenuous show of objectivity where the essence of the experience with which it deals is subjective.

The apparent objectivity of scientific procedure being the most powerful of paradigms in our modern culture, we are powerfully disposed to be persuaded by those accounts of human behaviour that it shapes. We are less disposed to ask the prior and fundamental question: is this a matter in which it is possible or desirable to achieve objectivity? It is my argument in this book that the desire for an unattainable objectivity is the key to many of the difficulties we have faced in formulating an adequate version of National Curriculum English. The quest for objectivity and certainties where none is to be found produces paradoxical results: that matters in which we (teachers and pupils) should trust our intuitive understanding are made both more complex and more shallow when we do not (the burdensome complexity of the 1990 National Curriculum Order for English being the immediately relevant example). If we are looking for wisdom and insight into sexuality and language we shall see more clearly through the simple words of some of Blake's short poems than we ever will through the 'expert' jargons of either *Cosmopolitan* or SEC:

> Never pain to tell thy love
> Love that never told can be;
> For the gentle wind does move

Silently, invisibly.

I told my love, I told my love,
I told her all my heart,
Trembling, cold, in ghastly fears –
Ah, she doth depart.

Soon as she was gone from me
A traveller came by
Silently, invisibly –
O, was no deny.

(Blake, 1976, p.161)

One looks away from Blake's poem with a disturbed sense of its having expressed more than one can rightly know, of there being something beyond its accessible meaning. The same can of course be said of any good poem; but here the mystery is part of the very subject matter. Blake summons up the image of the faceless but fatal intruder who, like the worm in 'The Sick Rose', spirits the cherished lover away. But this intruder is no external enemy, no melodramatic evil spirit over which the victim has no control. The loved one is lost through the unwise action of the speaker, who denied the wisdom whose point he now so clearly sees. The phrase 'Love that never told can be' embraces a triple wisdom: about the nature of human feeling, about the limits of human understanding and about the limits of language. Too determined an effort of consciousness, too insistent a drive to investigate and explain one's feelings risks the destruction of the feelings themselves. We are not made that way; we are not strong enough to bear the burden of our true selves. Something asks to be left unsaid. Love, says Blake, cannot truly be told. In the telling it may be corrupted. Words distort and corrode when pushed too relentlessly to explain and describe: 'We murder to dissect'. The traveller, in his silent and invisible way, is thus the inevitable result of a defiance of nature. He is a figure for that element in human relationships over which we can have no control – any more than we can over 'the gentle wind'.

If we compare Blake's English with the would-be objective language of *Cosmopolitan* or the SEC we feel we are moving between different countries of the mind. Blake's is truly the native language in the sense that he speaks with rather than against its idiomatic spirit: its rhythms are the familiar rhythms of spoken English and its vocabulary is one that we feel immediately at home in. Here is a man speaking to men and women like himself, in a shared language. The poem enacts the very reticence that the speakers had rejected. The poem does *not* tell all. What Blake 'knows about language' cannot be located within any taxonomy of knowledge. We cannot recast what he (and we) know, in the form of a principle. We experience that knowledge as recognition (re-cognition). It's as though Blake rehearses a truth of human experience that it is in our defective natures sometimes to forget. And here we encounter an important paradox: that Blake, by contemplating a fact of human experience, of human nature, with what T.S. Eliot called 'terrifying honesty', produces a poem with more claim to be called objective than the technical accounts of human behaviour with which I am here comparing it. Blake's poem stands in impersonal judgement on the pretensions of those contemporary examples – and of much more. There is no heart in the brave new world inhabited by *Cosmopolitan*'s robotic partners ('lovers' is too warm, too human a word) and by the automata conjured in SEC's repugnant vocabulary. But, of course, there is still heart in the real people – the lovers, the teachers, the children – who are travestied in that vocabulary. We are not yet beyond understanding Blake when he says 'I told her all my heart': the ancient, richly loaded word cannot be simply expunged, and neither can the insight it helps to express. It has the power of which Edward Thomas speaks: 'A great writer so uses the words of every day that they become a code of his own which the world is bound to learn and in the end take unto itself' (Thomas, 1993). For teachers of English this should be a source of strength, of resistance to orthodoxies such as established themselves in the eighties and eventually entrenched themselves in the National Curriculum – most particularly the orthodoxy of 'objective intelligence', which persuades 'human beings to identify themselves with no more than a narrow mode of perception' (the subject is the assessment of GCSE Oral Communication):

> The nature of the audience or listener will in turn have implications for the *'feedback'* which is given to the speaker – including monologue situations where the flow of *communication* is largely one-way. Even in these situations speakers depend on *signals* of attention, support, comprehension and interest from their audience, and skilled speakers will modify their speech to take account of indications that any of these are lacking. In *dialogue situations* – such as group discussions, interviews and other kinds of *conversation* – the feedback given by listeners will be central (and speakers will themselves also be listeners of course, as these *roles* change reciprocally). This creates additional problems of assessment; it may be difficult to determine whether an individual student's rather brief or relatively uninspiring performance was strongly influenced by the unsupportive contributions made by her or his partners in the situation.
>
> (SEC, 1986, p.41)

Here is prefigured the ugly behaviourist jargon that was to be so active in the 1989 Cox Report ('oracy involves teaching and assessing children's language behaviour with other people') and the 1990 Order. It survives in the 1995 requirement that children should be *'taught* to use gesture and intonation appropriately'. 'The word as sound', says the American critic and theologian Walter Ong, 'signals interiority and mystery (a certain inaccessibility even in intimacy)...the spoken word is somehow always radically inaccessible: it flees us, eludes our grasp, escapes when we try to immobilize it' (Ong, 1967). Ong's words stress the limits of our knowledge and control. The GCSE guide denies them. The price paid is the radical distortion of what (speaking and listening being considered proper objects of 'assessment') is ostensibly highly valued. This is Ted Hughes' 'objective intelligence...turning into stupidity'. To speak of 'feedback' being 'given to the speaker' is to disregard the fluidity of the relationship between speakers and listeners. The GCSE guide speaks of 'the complexity of the data which we process whenever we evaluate spoken language'. This of course extends the jargon of 'feedback' and 'signals' and sustains the delusion that we can for the purposes of 'evaluation' empty language of its substance. We cannot: if we are attending to *what* is being said, attending with that fullness of attention without which we cannot understand, then we are part of an experience: we are listening. We are not, like computers, 'processing data'. We cannot stand outside a process of which we are a part. Culture, says Theodore Roszak,

> often grows by metaphoric elaboration, one field of thought borrowing from another for suggestive images. But at a certain point, metaphorical elaboration becomes plain bad thinking. That point is where the metaphors stop being suggestive and are taken literally.
>
> (Roszak, 1986, p.44)

The SEC passage quoted above is 'plain bad thinking' of that kind. It reflects 'technological idolatry', a complicity with one of the most powerful currents running through the English language today: the current of idiom and feeling that has its roots in technological invention and change. Such a current, with its familiar irresistible momentum, tends to sweep aside the more slowly gathered images of humanity established in our culture. The technological idiom and inert rhythms of the passage quoted tend to promote a conception of human beings as mechanisms without inner lives, mechanisms whose 'performance' is amenable to systematic observation and control. With the curriculum itself under increasingly centralized control teachers would be invited to re-invent themselves as controllers in their turn: 'assessing language behaviours rather than actual output', 'checking product' and 'monitoring learning behaviour' (SEAC, 1990) (see chapter 6).

That prose of such a quality was addressed to teachers of English suggests why the eighties were in some ways an inauspicious time for the inauguration of National Curriculum English. An adequate public language was not available; or, more accurately perhaps, those charged with finding a language that would do justice to 'English' and its teaching did not sufficiently dissociate themselves from 'the direction and main channel in which the thoughts and interests of men were then flowing'. In the mid-eighties those thoughts and interests tended, at the level of public expression, to be penetrated by technical vocabularies drawn from industry, war and information technology: vocabularies in many ways unsuitable for the discussion of English and its literature. As central control of education intensified, the 'current of national tendency' seemed at times to engulf any adequate public language for the discussion of teaching and learning at any level. F.R. Leavis's warning turned out to be painfully apt:

> Technological change has marked cultural consequences. There is an implicit logic that will impose, if not met by creative intelligence and corrective purpose, simplifying and reductive criteria of human need and human good, and generate, to form the mind and spirit of civilization, disastrously false and inadequate conceptions of the *ends* to which science should be a means. This logic or drive is immensely and insidiously powerful...

> (Leavis, 1972, p.94)

The signs were everywhere. The government's Green Paper on Higher Education (HMSO 1985) might have been written to prove Leavis's thesis. It is moreover strikingly representative of the unpropitious climate in which the thinking about National Curriculum English would take place. In the Green Paper the word 'education' is largely drained of its traditional inwardness, its historical stress on the educing, the evolving of qualities of mind and spirit. The Green Paper's characteristic vocabulary was unsuited to any discussion of education that aims to go beyond utilitarian and pragmatic considerations of the present and foreseeable future. It was written in the language of industrial management and production: Higher Education's 'output of well-motivated graduates is vital to the country's economic performance'. Universities and public-sector institutions must 'adjust in a cost-effective way...to the developing need for skills-updating'. It is no surprise that the humanities, in their preoccupation with aesthetic, moral and spiritual questions that transcend the immediacies of present economic needs occupied a position somewhere between that of a luxury and a nuisance. What the Green Paper exhibited was the erosion of a moral vocabulary. The encompassing industrial terminology has political implications too. If we think of people as 'output' 'manpower' or 'product' subject to 'quality control' we more readily persuade ourselves that they should be 'well-motivated', which may too easily mean quiescent.

Matthew Arnold's words in *Culture and Anarchy* (1869) have lost none of their original force: 'The idea of perfection as an inward condition of the mind and spirit is at variance with the mechanical and material civilization in esteem with us' (Trilling, 1956). It seemed at times during the 1980s as though the only way in which qualities of mind and spirit could be recognized was by accommodating them (however blatant the incongruity) within the prevailing technical vocabularies. The key word was, and still is, 'skills'. There seemed to be no ability or quality this talismanic word (with its connotations of technical expertise) was not called upon to describe, from the 'dedication skills' of geriatric nurses to the 'commonsense skills' required in CPVE courses. One of the effects of so strained a usage was to convert elusive moral abstractions into fixed entities, thus creating the impression that it was appropriate and feasible that they should be assessed. 'The ability to work in a team'; 'to show sensitivity to the values of others'; 'to review one's own strengths and weaknesses' – these were amongst the 'Core Skills' that the National Curriculum Council wished to see assessed in A level subjects (NCC, 1990). Verbal sleight of hand repeatedly represented 'core skills' not as the abstractions they are but as concrete, tangible, measurable content: they were to be 'introduced', 'included', 'incorporated' into A level syllabuses – although in the event they never were.

The tyranny of the assessment systems that would dominate the first National Curriculum Order, sapping teachers' energies and morale, was directly attributable to this false philosophy. To persuade ourselves that the inherently subjective may be turned inside out for inspection, description and evaluation is to open the way for the atomizing, indigestibly wordy accounts of 'skills and competencies' of the Cox Report (1989) and the first National Curriculum Order for English (1990). Cox found nothing untoward, for instance, in the notion that 'the ability to listen actively [how else can one listen?] involves skills of concentration [an act of the whole mind] and assimilation'. The objection is not to an unhappy choice of expression. Such usage corrupts understanding and, as I argue later, distorts practice. Phrases such as 'writing skills' and 'oral skills' are now parts of the unquestioned vocabulary of 'English' (routinely entrenched by curricular documents and coursebooks alike) but they have not advanced our understanding.

Unsurprisingly, the official publications addressed to teachers of English in the mid-eighties showed the 'form and pressure' of the times. What was surprising was that often they showed little else. The reductively pragmatic language in which so much of the general debate about education was conducted penetrated the discussion of English to an alarming degree. To be a teacher of English in the eighties was often to feel estranged from the public language in which one was professionally addressed. In 1986 HMI set the tone for the discussions that would culminate in the first National Curriculum Order for English:

> The objectives of *English from 5 to 16* embraced kinds of language experience which pupils might be expected to have been given by common age points and expectations with regard to performance...it is possible for the profession to agree the broad categories of language experience which should be offered to pupils...these experiences will be delivered in lively and interesting ways.
>
> (DES, 1986, p.8)

The ugliness of the writing accurately reflects the denial of language as an inner possession. The prose feels undernourished, strained and cut off from its natural resources in English and its literature. The objectivity offered is spurious, 'experience' being, historically and in normal contemporary usage, heavy with the implication of subjectivity. It wrenches the language out of joint to speak of 'giving', 'offering', or 'delivering' an experience. The teacher's contribution, such an idiom implies, is habitually instrumental: he controls, he delivers, he observes. We are not looking at a mere infelicity of style. The image of the teacher is in a new and impersonal mould: a teacher with the ability (in the bizarre words of one academic linguist claiming teachers' attention) of 'mature educated native speakers to exercise full control over their native environment' (Carter and Burton, 1982).

The academic linguist there joins hands with the sex-counsellor. For what else are those *Cosmopolitan* partners doing as they strive for 'successful communication in sexual situations' if not attempting 'full control over their native environment by means of their language behaviour'? The truth is that such control is unattainable, an illusion. No matter how 'clear, specific and uncritical' they may be, nemesis awaits those robotic partners if they believe otherwise. Blake's awe in the face of language turns out to be practical as well as wise. Poets, novelists and dramatists are more likely to appreciate this than linguists – and teachers of English are more likely to learn from them too. We never quite know where we shall hear that 'different language, more direct and personal' that Calvino insisted was so necessary 'in an age of generic and abstract words' (Calvino, 1987), or where Leavis's 'creative intelligence and corrective purpose' will declare itself. They are there, it seems to me, in Tony Marchant's 1994 television play *Speaking in Tongues*.

It is a parable for the times. *Speaking in Tongues* is about lying. Very proficient lying. Lying habitually, routinely and successfully, for a living.

In the play earning a living by lying blends, fatally, into living a lie. In an inspired symbol of that confusion the principal liar works from home, indeed from her own living room. She earns her living by peddling 'telephone sex' fantasies. She is an expert: her routines are very polished, her sense of what her customers want acute, her overall 'performance' unnervingly persuasive. Or rather it would be if, since this is a television play, we couldn't see her as well as hear her. What we see is a domestic interior of an unremarkable kind. This is where she operates, where at the ringing of the phone she switches effortlessly into 'play' mode, whatever she was previously doing and whoever she was previously talking to. That means, usually, her husband. He is used to her breaking off when she has to. He is quite used to going about his own business whilst she is doing hers, bustling past her or sticking a mug of tea in her hand as she 'performs'. It is wonderfully funny: supporting the phone on her shoulder, she dunks a digestive biscuit in her tea in mid-fantasy flight and somehow manages to integrate the natural intakes of breath and the noise of masticated biscuit and slurped tea with the expertly simulated groans and coarse verbal enticements that are all part of the trade of 'talking dirty'. The dislocation of words and meaning is total. The meaning of what she is doing lies in why she is doing it. And that has nothing to do with sex. She does it, of course, for money. Her 'communication skills' are extraordinary and, for all its sighing and moaning lubriciousness, her English is standard. She is a good communicator, and she knows (as she would be required to know in the National Curriculum) 'how to match language to purpose and audience' and to 'reflect on her own performance'.

It looks like the recipe for easy money and easy living. One might expect her husband to see it in that light, for he makes his own living by telling a different kind of lie, socially completely acceptable. He peddles sanitized and embroidered images of the town's industrial, mining past for the benefit of visitors to the town's museum. Fatally, however, it begins to dawn upon him that there are occasions when the language he hears her using to excite the 'punters' overlaps with the language of endearment between himself and her. He cannot believe in the dissociating mechanism on which earning her living depends. He cannot accept that the words don't necessarily mean the same thing in totally different contexts. He comes to believe that his wife must be giving more of herself through those supposedly 'professional', technically effective words than she claims. Whether or not she is, the insight is a true one and its outcome predictable: he loses his self-control and kills her. We are not the sole possessors and controllers of the words we use. They have their emotional histories, their roots in the life of the feelings. 'That was lovely', she says to him after they have made love. But 'lovely' is a soiled word. He has heard it once too often in her professional repertoire of verbal tricks. Is she living a lie with him? How can he tell? Words have effects beyond those we may intend them to have. Our control is always limited. There can be no strict 'match', ever, between 'language' and 'situation and purpose'. Blake's 'invisible traveller' comes in many guises.

CHAPTER THREE
A Language of Conviction

It is easy to forget that the penetration of technical and materialist vocabularies into every area of public life is of fairly recent origin. Its very success makes it seem natural. As Donald Davie has said, we are all 'subject to a daily and hourly bombardment of language from innumerable sources which characteristically...transform human or moral transactions into technological or financial or behaviouristic terms' (Greenbaum (Ed.), 1985). It would be surprising if education were to remain immune to those vocabularies and the modes of thinking they reflect. 'The machinery of education', said F.R. Leavis, 'works in with the modern world' (Leavis and Thompson, 1933). It is an irony of the present time that as education (with 'English' as part of it) has become more centralized the public language which it draws on and consolidates has grown increasingly eccentric. Both Arnold and Leavis, in their reminders that 'mind and spirit' cannot be accommodated within – but can be traduced by – materialist vocabularies, represent a widespread consciousness of what is at stake. However, a full half-century after *Culture and Anarchy* a government-appointed committee on the teaching of 'English' could still avail itself unselfconsciously of a public language that would have met with Arnold's approval. Like the linguist quoted earlier, the Newbolt Committee had views on 'language' 'environment' and 'control'. The differences, though, are radical. What lay to hand or, more precisely, what bound the members of that committee, was a language of conviction: a language that drew its strength and its persuasive force from a set of inherited and attested assumptions about the moral importance of a language and its literature in the life of a nation:

> English is not merely the medium of our thought, it is the very stuff and process of it. It is itself the English mind, the element in which we live and work. In its full sense it connotes not merely acquaintance with a certain number of terms, or the power of spelling these terms correctly and arranging them without gross mistakes. It connotes the discovery of the world by the first and most direct way open to us, and the discovery of

ourselves in our native environment. And as our discoveries become successively wider, deeper, and subtler, so should our control of the instrument which shapes our thought become more complete and exquisite, up to the limit of artistic skill. For the writing of English is essentially an art, and the effect of English literature in education is the effect of an art upon the development of human character.

(HMSO, 1921, p.20)

There, Newbolt speaks out of the powerful tradition of understanding to which it is indebted for its confident tones. 'Environment' tends nowadays to be used in a purely material sense. With Newbolt, however, it is a word that embraces both the inner and the outer worlds. Language is the chief way in which the two are united, the chief way in which we inhabit the world into which we are born. We have no choice in that respect. We live and work in a native language from which we cannot escape; it shapes our thoughts and feelings, places limits on our understanding. Thus – and this is Newbolt's most important point – the quality of our thoughts and feelings, the depth of our understanding, will be very much a matter of the quality and depth of the language we experience. Certain conclusions for the teaching and learning of English inevitably follow. Newbolt speaks of

...English in the highest sense, that it is the channel of *formative culture* for all English people, and the medium of the creative art by which all English writers of distinction, whether poets, historians, philosophers or men of science, have secured for us the power of *realising* some part of their own experience of life.

(HMSO, 1921, p.12)

The use of the word 'realise' here is crucial and clarifies the nature of those 'discoveries' of which the first passage quoted speaks with such forceful conviction. In 'realising some part of their own experience of life', we make it more probable that we shall be able to 'realise our own impressions and communicate them to others'. The culture of which those writers are a part will thus be formative: our range of feeling, our sensibility, will be the richer for their influence. None of Newbolt's key words is open to precise definition; the appeal is, implicitly, to experience.

The first passage I have quoted is preceded by this:

It is a common experience that to find fit language for our impressions not only renders them clear and definite to ourselves and to others, but in the process leads to deeper insight and fresh discoveries, at once explaining and extending our knowledge.

(HMSO, 1921, p.20)

Few surely would now doubt this. What many are unpersuaded of, however, is the organic connection between the making of those 'fresh discoveries' through literature and 'our control of the instrument which shapes our thought'. For Newbolt such control arises out of dealing with the writing of English as 'essentially an art'; for the National Curriculum Council in 1992 it lay in definition: in the revised Order 'Attainment Target 3' should 'offer a clear definition of basic writing skills, the grammatical knowledge pupils must master if they are to become effective writers, and the variety of ways in which competence can be developed' (NCC, 1992).

The 'control' exhibited in Newbolt's own prose is an interesting test of its claims for English as an art. Clearly that control cannot be explained in terms of 'skills'. It is itself the demonstration of 'formative culture'. We feel (even before we look for specific influences) the presence of the strong language of understanding that Newbolt has absorbed and which gives the tone to its argument. It is a governing assumption of this understanding that in matters of language we cannot separate the moral and the technical. Speaking of 'the effect of English literature in education' as 'the effect of an art upon the development of human character' Newbolt is far from adopting the moralizing posture these words might now suggest. The words are rooted in a conception of language as embodying the moral and spiritual history of the civilization within which it has developed: of language (in Seamus Heaney's beautiful phrases) as essential to 'the intricate and various foliage of history and culture' that we 'grow up beneath' (Heaney, 1988). Dignity naturally accrues to teachers conscious of the implication that a pupil will come under two influences: 'the creative power of the author whose record he is studying, and the appreciative judgement of the teacher who is introducing him to the intimacy of a greater intellect' (HMSO, 1921).

Behind the Newbolt Report we feel the pressure of a common sensibility, a sensibility with strong nineteenth-century roots. The strength of those roots makes the report proof against that mode of materialist study which, shirking judgement, seeks to reduce men and their works to mere expressions of the Zeitgeist or of their social origins. No one can dispute 'the impetus given to [Newbolt's] arguments by the war of 1914–1918' (Baldick, 1983) and, though it may seem Utopian to hope that 'through English we may find more easily the way to bridge the social chasms which now divide us' (HMSO, 1921), Newbolt's assertions of the 'common right to an education of this kind', 'the common discipline and enjoyment of it', have led on to practices that strongly contradict the élitism of which it has routinely been accused. There could, for Newbolt, be no argument for limiting the opportunities of native speakers to enter upon their native possession ('the element in which we live and work') more widely and deeply.

That common sensibility was until quite recently intensely active in the teaching of English. In order to understand the implications of its displacement (not least through the National Curriculum) it is necessary to appreciate the moral and social philosophy by which it was shaped: a philosophy within which we can locate the origins of that rich, integrated conception of literacy found in the Newbolt Report. We hear the keynote of this philosophy in Coleridge's celebrated distinction between 'civilization' and 'cultivation'. 'A nation' was more fitly to

> be called a varnished than a polished 'people'; where this civilization is not grounded in cultivation, in the harmonious development of those qualities and faculties that characterize our humanity. We must be men in order to be citizens.

> (Coleridge, 1972, p.33)

Here Coleridge gives us a standard by which to judge all moral, political and educational enterprises, as well as the language in which they are conducted. To Coleridge the language was variously healthy or diseased in the degree to which it reflected and promoted that 'harmonious development'. Thus 'deep thinking is only attainable by a man of deep feeling'; the profoundest imprints in the language were made by men of whom this was outstandingly true. Hence the vital place of Shakespeare in the 'harmonious development' both of individuals and of 'civilization'. 'Drawn from the profoundest depths of his moral being', Shakespeare's language expresses a sensibility in which thought and feeling, imagination and intuition are compact – harmoniously developed indeed. (What better reason could there be for the inclusion of Shakespeare in a national curriculum?) Shakespeare was inevitably central to Coleridge's passionately held view of a developed language as 'a magnificent History of acts of individual mind, sanctioned by the collective mind of the country'. For Coleridge, to recognize the dynamic relationship between the 'individual mind' and the 'collective mind' was to acknowledge that critical obligations fall to those who understand what it means to 'abuse' the language: 'what is it that I employ my metaphysics on?...to expose the folly and legerdemain of those who [thus] abuse the sacred organ of language'. There would always be plenty to hinder that 'harmonious development' (White, 1938).

To Coleridge it was axiomatic that 'the inward man' could not be other than intimately affected by the quality of his reading. He was prepared – in a strikingly modern phrase – to 'judge the average health of the consumers by the articles of greatest consumption'. With the growth of what Coleridge himself called 'the reading public' the educational and social challenge was inescapable. It was not enough that children should simply be taught to read and write (he was a vigorous opponent of the utilitarian ideas of the day). What had to be constantly borne in mind was that 'harmonious development' which education should promote: 'truly education...consists in educing the faculties and forming the habits'. We can imagine Coleridge's reaction to the modern teacher-critic who is prepared to devote a whole book to the proposition that 'the emotional satisfaction that children and young people gained from reading material that was not highly regarded was none the less as "genuine" as that supposedly offered to the few by "literature"' (Sarland, 1991). Obviously if emotional satisfaction – rather than harmonious development – is a sufficient aim, anything goes: as indeed it does in the research reported, all kinds of trash (including pornography) finding their way into the classroom. Regretting 'our Leavisite inheritance', the writer finds that it has 'almost inextricably confused moral and aesthetic values'. What to the modern critic are the elements of an inextricable confusion are to Coleridge the naturally combining aspects of 'harmonious development'. Within the tradition I am sketching here the distinction between moral and aesthetic – certainly as far as language is concerned – is meaningless. Its major exponents constantly stress (increasingly with a sense that such understanding is under serious threat) the unity of sensibility as the mark of a civilized mind.

We hear the representative voice of this tradition in George Eliot, who could not think of her own writing apart from the social and moral function it fulfilled: 'I will never write anything to which my whole heart, mind and conscience don't consent'. *Romola,* to which she was referring, she described as 'having been written with my best blood, such as it is, and with the most ardent care for veracity of which my nature is capable' (Haight, 1985). George Eliot there voices no mere opinion but an active principle of her being: she could not dissociate the action of her own sensibility ('heart, mind and conscience') from the effects she envisaged arising from it. She regarded it as axiomatic that her work should have 'a moral effect' on her readership, that it might be an 'instrument of culture', might 'call forth tolerant judgement, pity and sympathy' (Haight, 1985). The force of George Eliot's conviction that the creative artist takes 'a very large share in the quantum of human good' is equalled by that with which she expresses her fears at the morally degenerating effects of bad writing – whether writing which wishes to be taken as art ('a nasty mind makes nasty art') or the kind of popular writing (e.g. newspaper scandal) that threatens that 'moral wealth...which it has been the work of ages to produce' (Haight, 1985).

To George Eliot that 'moral wealth' was no less real than the idea of language as 'a magnificent History' was to Coleridge. The wealth was concentrated in 'the language of cultivated nations', permeating the minds and spirits of its speakers and writers in the natural way she so memorably evoked in referring to that 'union which binds men's affections, imagination, wit, and humour with the subtle implications of historical language' (Eliot, 1990, p.128). From this magnificent and inspiring conception arises the magnanimity which, accepting that 'the contemplation of whatever is great is itself religion and lifts us out of our egoism', could respond to the liturgical language of the Anglican church with a profound sense of what she inherited from the spiritual striving of previous generations. For Coleridge the Bible had been 'the main lever by which the moral and intellectual character of Europe has been raised to its present comparative height'. He had been profoundly exercised by what he saw as its diminishing influence. George Eliot lacked Coleridge's unequivocal faith, and yet:

> What an age of earnest faith, grasping a noble conception of life and determined to bring all things into harmony with it has recorded itself in the simple, pregnant, rhythmical English of those collects and of the Bible.
>
> (Haight, 1985, p.265)

The continuing activity of so 'noble' a 'conception' in the currency of English itself represents (in Coleridge's phrase) 'a collation of the present with the past'. It cannot be disavowed, though it can of course be devalued or misunderstood. Newbolt would register the diminishing familiarity of the English people with 'the one great piece of literature which for centuries gave something of a common form, a common dignity to the thoughts and speech of the people' (HMSO, 1921). However, in words strikingly reminiscent of those George Eliot used to describe the sensibility *Romola* grew from, Newbolt said that the Bible 'has gone down into the emotional life of the nation and has been effectual in a thousand ways in the words, thoughts and instinctive actions of that life'. 'It is in everything that we see, hear, feel because it is in us, in our blood'.

Matthew Arnold's lofty aspirations for the moral effects of literature – 'the greatest power available in education' (Sutherland (ed.), 1973) – are now easily scorned. However, behind his description of its language as 'a nation's great instrument of thought' is the inclusiveness of Coleridge's and George Eliot's conception: thought and feeling, the possibilities for spiritual development, the quality of our perceptions could not be dissociated from, and were largely dependent upon, the quality of the language available to us. When Arnold spoke of the need to 'keep up our communications with the future' it was with a sense (shared with Coleridge and George Eliot) that there was likely to be much in it that would threaten to sever its 'communications' with the past: 'with the best that has been known and said in the world: the history of the human spirit' (Arnold, 1873). Arnold wrote both as a critic of contemporary culture and as a schools inspector acutely aware that its values were bound to deeply influence educational beliefs and practices. Thus, like Coleridge and George Eliot, he spoke with prescient force of the consequences for 'the inward man' of levels of literacy raised just enough to render people vunerable to its abuses. 'Plenty of people', he said in *Culture and Anarchy*, 'will try to give the masses, as they call them, an intellectual food prepared and adapted in the way they think proper for the actual condition of the masses' (Trilling, 1956). Hence Arnold's animadversions against the Revised Code of 1862 – an early national curriculum – which recall Coleridge in stressing that 'mechanical instruction' in reading was useless unless grounded in 'general intellectual cultivation'. Coleridge's 'harmonious development' (of society and individual alike) would be impossible if schools were seen only as 'mere machines for reading, writing and arithmetic', rather than as 'living wholes with complex functions, religious, moral and intellectual' (Sutherland (Ed.), 1973).

What above all unites Coleridge, Arnold and George Eliot within the tradition I am sketching here is their fundamental conviction that we can say little that is important about language (and, by extension, the teaching of English), unless we acknowledge that it is an inner possession. If *Romola* was written with George Eliot's 'best blood' it was, as Newbolt's echoing metaphor proclaims, partly 'our blood'; George Eliot, that is, herself partook of the 'emotional life of the nation' into which the Bible had 'gone down'. The objection now might be that we can no longer persuade ourselves that we live in the culturally homogeneous society implied in Newbolt's use of the word 'our'; that the multiplicity of ethnic groups, cultures, religions and languages contained within contemporary British society makes it impossible, insulting even, to suggest that they are of one 'blood'. And yet, in so far as children from non-British cultures come into possession of the English language through education, they too partake of the 'emotional life' that is in it. Of course, the morally confident vocabulary upon which Coleridge and George Eliot could draw was rooted in the larger confidence of a culture and a readership to which that vocabulary was readily intelligible. The confidence has gone; the vocabulary is either vanished or enfeebled: no public report on the teaching of English will ever again speak, as Newbolt could, of 'the three great natural affections of the human spirit – the love of truth, the love of beauty, and the love of righteousness. Man loves all these by nature and for their own sake only' (HMSO, 1921). And yet the Bible is still demonstrably there, like Shakespeare, in a vast range of phrase and idiom that is daily drawn upon by people who love both as well as by those who have little respect for either. That range is an aspect of what, contemplating the history of English literature, F.R. Leavis called 'a full continuity of mind, spirit and sensibility – which is what we desperately need' (Leavis, 1969). As Leavis's final phrase indicates, that continuity could not be taken for granted. Under modern conditions ('the machinery of education works in with the modern world') it was all too likely to be disregarded, devalued or despised. 'Continuity' (Leavis's variation on Coleridge's 'collation of the present upon the past' and Arnold's keeping up 'our communications with the future') depended upon an appreciation of

> the nature of the existence of English literature, a living whole that can have its life only in the living present, in the creative response of individuals, who collaboratively renew and perpetuate what they participate in – a cultural community of consciousness.
>
> (Leavis, 1962)

The educational implications can be put concretely thus: when we read, see or discuss a Shakespeare play, we gain access to a consciousness that, by virtue of our inwardness with the common language, we incorporate, make more our own. In so far as we really come alive to Macbeth's agonies of indecision or to Lear's self-discovery we strengthen our hold on the moral resources of the language, we 'feel into' (Leavis's phrase) the deep relations between our individual selves and the culture that has helped and is continuing to help to form them. This is the culture that Leavis said 'transcends the individual as the language he inherits transcends him' (Leavis and Thompson, 1933). Within it we find 'a sense of relative value and a memory – such wisdom as constitutes the residuum of general experience'.

Leavis there conceives the relations between the individual, the native language and the culture very much along Coleridgean lines. For Leavis, as for Coleridge and his nineteenth-century successors, that sense of relative value commits anyone who shares the view to the making of judgements. If we are convinced (as they all were) that 'the debasement of language is not merely a matter of words; it is the debasement of emotional life and the quality of living' (Leavis and Thompson, 1933) we have to know what we are talking about. We have to be able to demonstrate that to speak of the 'living subtlety of the finest idiom' is not empty phrase-making. Without such a conviction we are unlikely to have what Leavis said was needed in education, as never before: 'energy, disinterestedness and firm consciousness of function' (Leavis and Thompson, 1933).

By the time it came to be articulated in this way, that 'firm consciousness' had already become difficult to focus: difficult, but not impossible. We find it a generation or more later in the early work of David Holbrook. In the hands of Holbrook, a poet and novelist as well as a literary critic and teacher, the Coleridgean idea of words as 'living powers', as a force for good or evil, lives on, most especially in the greatly influential *English for Maturity* (1961). Holbrook acknowledges his indebtedness to *English for the English* (1921) by George Sampson, who was a member of the Newbolt Committee. For Holbrook, as for Sampson, the English teacher's responsibility was not limited to the technical; technical command would develop within the more general education of sensibility. There is an echo of this idea in the 1995 Order's stipulation that literature in school should 'extend pupils' ideas and their moral and emotional understanding' but it strikes us there as not much more than a form of words. As I suggest in later chapters, it is not an idea that penetrates and shapes National Curriculum English as a whole. It is not rooted in the quality of understanding we find in Holbrook's view of the way English may 'develop that richness of the individual being which releases sympathy and creative energy in community':

> This is achieved by the arts: and it was to them civilised and leisured communities of the past gave their effort – to coming together in submission to embodiments of the human spirit. It is by these that men come to possess their traditions and values – possess them in their thought and feeling, rather than as acquired fragments of knowledge about them. And we possess our traditions largely through and in *the word*.
>
> (Holbrook, 1961, pp.17–18)

'Knowledge *about* language' (a development that Holbrook's phrase 'fragments of knowledge about them' foreshadows) cannot be a substitute for that 'relish for the English word' which it is the business of English teaching to create. The creation of such a relish is indissociable from the cultivation of literacy: 'The way to develop one's mastery over English is to live within a rich context of its lively use, by reading, listening and talking' (Holbrook, 1961). How simple this is in its integral view of those three elements; in its recognition that our reading, as part of the education of sensibility, will have its inevitable effect on the way we express ourselves and respond to others in our speech. This integral view (as I show in chapters 6 and 7) is what we urgently need to restore; the divisions of both National Curriculum Orders have severely undermined it.

In stressing that teachers should themselves be educated in the best that the culture has to offer, that they need to appreciate the link between continuous acquaintance with imaginative work (that 'rich context' had to be 'a context of its imaginative use') and the individual's own growing powers, Holbrook was still able to draw upon widely shared cultural assumptions. The most important of those assumptions was that civilized literacy would only arise from acting upon Ezra Pound's view of the 'function' of literature: 'it has to do with the clarity and vigour of "any and every" thought and opinion. It has to do with maintaining the very cleanliness of the tools, the health of the very matter of thought itself' (Leavis and Thompson, 1933). *English for Maturity* accordingly shows how a concern with language must go beyond language; it demonstrates in its scrupulous attention to the English of our best writers the intimate connections between thought, perception and feeling. Chapter 4 ('The very Culture of the Feelings') is something of a *locus classicus* in the tradition to which it belongs. If we wish to know, concretely, what it means to speak of 'the word – the complex, sinewy, subtle and evasive word' as being 'at one with our life', we can follow Holbrook in his memorable analysis of Wordsworth's sonnet on the death of his daughter Catherine:

> Surpris'd by joy – impatient as the wind
> I turned to share the transport – Oh! with whom
> But Thee, deep buried in the silent tomb,
> The spot which no vicissitude can find?

Having read Holbrook's account (showing how 'the poem *does what it says* in the opening lines, and thus re-enacts the experience in us'), it is difficult to imagine anyone resisting his conclusion that the poem 'propagates sympathy by making us more aware of the inward life of others...You cannot make "the whole man" a civilized being by ratiocinative means alone'. Holbrook was nevertheless keenly aware (the passionate, combative tone of his writing reflects it) that such conviction was already under threat; that the heartless, mechanistic language of which I gave instances in chapter 2 was already gaining a hold. His warnings about the pretensions of the 'communications experts' have lost none of their relevance in the era of the National Curriculum: 'what too often they leave out of account is our communication with ourselves, in the inward world with which we must first learn to deal before we can deal with the outside world'. Such 'experts', he said, 'really seem to act as if human beings are a form of rather inefficient thinking machine'; they often 'fail to see the mystery of the flesh that can think and be aware of its existence' (Holbrook, 1961).

A language of conviction does survive. Reviewing Colin Evans' *English People – The Experience of Teaching and Learning English in British Universities* (1993), Ian Robinson expressed surprise that so many of the undergraduates 'interviewed still take for granted or yearn for the Arnold–Newbolt–Leavis kind of attachment to literature: "I always open a book with great excitement. I walk around Dillons in a state of ecstasy. It's someone's soul between the covers. It is something very, very exciting"' (Evans, 1993). Robinson noted 'the strong survival' amongst the students 'of Arnold–Newbolt assumptions about the role of literature and literary education in modern civilization' (Robinson, 1994). 'In a rampantly instrumental society', says one student, 'you will turn to something else for solace or ultimate value, and literature is that'. These are hardly fashionable words (*'solace'* says Robinson, 'is pure Arnold') and they are as unlikely as words such as 'excitement', 'soul' and 'ecstasy' to find their way into the work of committees deliberating and prescribing for English teaching in schools. They are, as we have seen, nonetheless words with strong roots. That they sprang to the lips of Colin Evans' respondents proves the continuing power of the tradition to which they belong. It is a language of conviction that has survived against the odds. It has withstood not only the increasingly bleak public language in which the 'nation's great instrument of thought' has come to be discussed but also degrees of indifference, incomprehension and hostility within the English teaching profession itself. It is not possible to understand the climate in which the public language of 'English' took shape in the National Curriculum without examining key elements of the 'professional language' in the years that preceded it. Colin Evans' respondents prove David Holbrook's idea of 'English' to be still active in the nineties; in the previous two decades, however, that idea came under the strenuous and concerted challenge that was bound eventually to leave very deep imprints in National Curriculum English.

Torbe and Protherough's *Classroom Encounters: Language and English Teaching* (1977) consisted of articles originally published in the journal of the National Association for the Teaching of English and showed the nature of the challenge very clearly. The editors' introduction juxtaposed two previously published accounts of classroom practice so as to give readers a clear view of recent advances in understanding the English teacher's function. The first is taken from *Patterns of Learning* (1973):

> ...a class of fifteen-year-old pupils; they are just settling into their seats in the room where the films are shown...Not wanting to overstructure responses the teacher keeps his introduction brief...When everyone is seated the lights go out and the film starts...
>
> The lights go up, the teacher briefly reminds the pupils that he would like them to talk over their impressions...and that perhaps they would like to make further notes. The small groups form up in different parts of the room

and talking begins...

Now the groups have settled. The teacher sits in on one and listens to the discussion. On the whole he is contented just to listen as the pupils respond personally to the film...The teacher moves on to another group...and yet another...After about twenty-five minutes of discussion the teacher calls the class together for a larger discussion...

The discussion has now more or less exhausted itself and the teacher, sensing that little further learning would take place, suggests that the class might like once more to see the film...

Whatever the impressions stirred, the teacher now asks the pupils to try and write about them. The choice is, in a sense, infinite. This being so, the teacher feels there must be opportunities to write in whatever form each pupil senses appropriate...He therefore gives the pupils the choice of writing a poem, a piece of prose (perhaps an opening to a short story, or a vignette) a dramatization, even an account of the processes involved while responding to the film and in the subsequent discussions...

(Stratta *et al.*, 1973, reproduced in Torbe and Protherough, 1977, p.7)

The second comes from *English versus Examinations* (1965):

The teacher reads aloud some carefully chosen passage of prose or verse. If prose, he reads perhaps six pages...if verse something complete in itself, longer than a sonnet but usually less than a hundred lines...something which few of them know already, but which they may come to enjoy with profit. Swift, Jane Austen, Lawrence (poems), Hardy (poems), Keats, Jefferies, and Conrad are all good sources.

Next a part of the passage is read again in fairly short sections, but in each case a word or phrase is omitted and some other word (usually less apt) is substituted, the change being indicated by a change in the reader's voice...The pupils are asked to jot down what they judge (or remember) to be the original word. For instance, if the poem were *Kubla Khan* (though for many classes it would be too familiar) 'screaming' might be substituted for 'wailing' in line 16, and 'constant' for 'ceaseless' in line 17. The words jotted down are in each case discussed by the class before the next section is given...Thus 'ceaseless' may lead to the nature and use of onomatopoeia and alliteration in the given context.

The two main advantages of this type of lesson are
1   a detective interest since there is in a limited sense a 'right' answer
2   the opportunity of discussing words, phrases, rhythms and imagery and all other such matters in an adequate context.

(O'Malley, 1965, reproduced in Torbe and Protherough, 1977, p.8)

These two teachers are described as 'both first-rate – memorable innovators', who 'led their generations'. They are united by a common professionalism, despite their 'different purposes' and their 'fundamentally different assumptions'. And yet, as one weighs those representative passages and the editors' commentary, those differences come to appear much *too* fundamental. It is difficult to avoid the conclusion that a 'professionalism' that can find room for both is no professionalism at all. What confronts us, very illuminatingly, in those passages is a collision of values which, as it moved towards partial resolution in the late 1970s and 1980s, would leave 'English' struggling to sustain its identity as a distinctive subject of the curriculum.

It is not easy to find a focus in the first passage. Certainly it is not the nature and value of the film. If anything it is the classroom procedures and 'processes' to which its showing gives rise. We are being led around whatever learning is going on rather than to its centre – much as the teacher goes around the groups in that half-reverential, tentative, apologetic way. He seems to be in retreat rather than in control: 'not wanting to overstructure responses' he is 'brief'; he 'would *like* them to talk over their impressions'; 'perhaps they would *like* to make further notes', he is 'contented just to listen'; they 'might *like*' to see the film again. It seems in a way immensely civilized. Certainly it suggests a remarkable degree of civility and understanding amongst those fifteen year olds: that they are aware of and happy to accept their teacher's very limited contribution to what is going on; that they share his trust in the value of their impressions; that, since it's a question of responding personally to the film, there is little for him to do other than to dispense warm acceptance of their responses and impressions. It is in the nature of the 'processes involved while responding to the film' that he cannot know what it will be most valuable for his students to write about. Just as it appeared that he had little more to rely on than his 'sensing that little further learning was taking place', so he depends on a corresponding intuitiveness in his pupils. 'The choice is, in a sense, infinite' – whatever the 'pupil senses appropriate'. The absence of information for the reader is matched by the contented detachment of the teacher – what Torbe and Protherough call 'a kind of educational negative capability'.

There is no infinity of choice – in any sense – for the second teacher here (a teacher very much in the Newbolt tradition). There is the recognized range of great writers to be visited and explored. Indeed, this is the 'fundamental assumption' informing his teaching: that there is a content to 'English' which is worth introducing to the young, that the choice to be made by the teacher is a matter of his own educated judgement, and that his purpose is to encourage the development of judgement in his pupils. That this development is taking place in the context of material chosen by the teacher on cultural grounds is of the essence. Dignity for the teacher lies in his superior knowledge and his intelligent capacity for deciding how he shall introduce his pupils to those parts of it that they may 'come to enjoy with profit'. It is, comparatively, a highly focused lesson; one based, moreover, on an obvious confidence in the English teacher's function. We can easily see the grounds on which this teacher might make out a case for his 'professionalism'. Can we say the same for the first? The commentators are in no doubt. This teacher, who seems to make an art of abstention or withdrawal, is in fact 'as informed, professional and committed as any teacher in the past'. Now of course this may be true; there are, as those words admit, comparisons to be made. The past is there, a possession of our minds, a range of achievements that we can readily document and that we can invoke in order to test the claims made for this latter-day teacher's professionalism. Curiously, however, the whole tenor of the commentators' remarks (and here they merely typify a set of contemporary attitudes) reflects either a lack of enthusiasm for or (at one extreme) an indifference to the past. Their prose communicates a sense that the period they and other teachers of 'English' were living through promised a euphoric release. It turns out to be much easier to see what the release is *from* rather than what it is *for.* This teacher doesn't see himself as 'a possessor of knowledge and expertise' but rather as 'a facilitator constructing contexts for his pupils to learn in, without predetermining all the time what it is that they do learn'. But surely all such constructions have to arise from a plan, to reflect some overall purpose; they must surely be shaped by beliefs somewhat more substantial than 'beliefs about the nature of talk and the way groups operate'. Perhaps, though, 'beliefs' is a more appropriate word than 'knowledge'; it certainly seems to belong more obviously within the longer description of the teacher as one who has

> shifted his attention away from the notion of a pre-planned syllabus to which the pupil is fitted, Procrustes-like, towards a more step-by-step process in which the teacher listens seriously to what each pupil has to say and adjusts his curriculum to what he sees as the necessary directions.
>
> (Torbe and Protherough, 1977, p.12)

'Seriously', 'adjusts', 'necessary': the words in themselves might lead us to expect exactitude and clarity in such a teacher's vision of his work and his relationship with his pupils. What exactly is meant by 'a step-by-step process' is not made clear but there is no doubt that the teacher's submissiveness, his delicacy even, in holding himself back has behind it a version of English in which 'the relationship of mutuality between teacher and taught...leaves the child the final arbiter of his own learning – in school as he has always been out of school' (Dixon, 1975). The implication that learning outside school, where there are no teachers, should be the model for learning inside school, where there obviously are, signifies a wish to blur or abolish such divisions, to prosecute an idea of learning in which boundaries set by institutions, by subject disciplines and by traditions of value and practice are as far as possible erased. As this idea was expressed in John Dixon's influential *Growth Through English*, Procrustes' victims were neither stretched nor cut down to size: the very bed seemed to have been abolished:

> What is English? It proves impossible to mark out an area less than the sum total of the planned and unplanned experiences through language by means of which a child gains control of himself and the surrounding world.
>
> (Dixon, 1975)

What is so astonishing is that results so solid (indeed breathtaking: what could it mean to 'gain control' of oneself 'and the surrounding world'?) should be capable of achievement through means so indeterminate: that such control could be achieved not through cultivating traditions of study that enable us to take stock of and absorb the lessons of the past, but by dispensing with them! This resolute contemporaneity – the conviction that, however inscrutable its processes may be, there is a principle of self-determination within individual children upon whose natural workings teachers may rely to produce learning – results in language of the elusiveness I am considering here. The very mistrust of the past weakens that habit which we traditionally regard as the mark of an educated mind: that it tests the intelligibility and value of its own language, its own expression, by looking beyond itself. If we ask what are the teacher's shaping values, the only available answer deepens the feeling of disorientation: 'It is how pupils actually do use language rather than any notion of how they *ought* to use it that controls both the shape of his teaching and his attempts to help them use it more successfully' (Torbe and Protherough, 1977).

The only clarity to be found in this is negative: the italicized *'ought'* signifies disapproval of the idea that it is the proper business of the teacher to make judgements. But if the teacher is not allowed to do that, what will it be that 'controls' and 'shapes' his teaching? What will the criteria for 'success' be? That hesitant, self-effacing stance, the reluctance to intrude, turns out to be no more than the logical expression of a deeper withdrawal: from commitment, from that sense of relative value that comes from the assimilation of and reflection upon a cultural tradition. Where such a tradition is mentioned it is only for its comparatively minor significance to be underlined: 'The underpinnings of his teaching rationale are not derived solely from external legitimation – "culture", "our heritage" – but also from a recognition of the realities of children's language, and the way young people interact with each other and with adults' (Torbe and Protherough, 1977).

The condescending inverted commas are as significant as the phrase 'external legitimation'. The phrase suggests that 'culture' and 'heritage' are to be regarded in no other light than as forms of oppression from which learners must be freed. There is no room for the human element, for the surely indisputable fact that it is partly through the assimilation of the 'culture' and the 'heritage' into which we are born that we come to know what it is to be human. 'The realities of children's language' are not a solid, pristine force of nature to be protected from 'cultural' influence. Already they are penetrated by it. However, the rhetoric bearing upon the presentation of this false opposition was a powerful one at the time. It is in John Dixon's statement that 'Learners are born free but are everywhere in chains' and in James Britton's reflections on 'the difficulty with a subject-centred role for educators':

> it throws off their shoulders the burden of deciding *what is to be learned* and the burden is likely to land nowhere. The fact that a teacher is interested in and has expert knowledge of 'a particular selection from the world' provides no evidence as to whether that selection will be of value to one, some or all of the children for whom he is responsible.
>
> (Britton, 1975, p.186)

For all Britton's obvious humanity, this is heartless. He seems to be asking teachers to invent the world anew, to decide (on what basis he doesn't say) what *will* be of value and, in so deciding, not to be influenced by those collected valuations, those shapings and selections of experience that we call 'subjects'. Obviously those shapings and selections are not constants: the recent history of 'English' as an academic subject in Higher Education is strong proof. But – the key point – organized methods of interpreting the inner and outer worlds serve their proper turn when they give us clear contexts within which to determine our own directions. Those methods, contrary to what Britton says, *are* the evidence of value: that, incontrovertibly, there are traditions of poetry, of musical composition, of historiography and so on is evidence that successions of minds have found those traditions hospitable to their own creative needs and powers – just as listeners and readers have in their turn. Of course, if we are looking for material, statistical, produceable 'evidence' of the value of any subject (particularly in the arts) we are unlikely to find it. The fallacy is to move from a recognition of the difficulty to the conclusion that, thus, there is no value. This is the drift towards nihilism. We see it in the Bullock Report (Britton was a member of the committee that produced it) where it is accepted that 'there is no evidence that the reading of literature in schools produces in any way the social or emotional effects claimed for it'. The committee could as a result find nothing more inspiring to say about the place of literature in the teaching of English than that it had 'value as a personal resource': 'Books compensate for the difficulties of growing up' (DES, 1975). Bullock's readiness to accept the language of the behavioural psychologist as adequate to the discussion of the arts in education is a token of its shallowness. If we look for *evidence* of 'social or emotional effects' we shall very obviously be disappointed. For we shall be looking for the wrong thing. Rather than acknowledge the moral argument for literature (an argument that has not until the present time ever been conducted in materialistic terms), the Bullock Committee simply acted as though they had never heard of it.

And yet, though Bullock may simply have spoken for the age in this respect – we all recognize the difficulty of finding a shared moral language – our need for a language of conviction survives. Torbe and Protherough's exemplary teacher may have little faith in 'culture' and 'our heritage'; 'there is' nonetheless 'underpinning everything, a clear rationale to which the teacher assimilates whatever seems needful and important' (Torbe and Protherough, 1977). The moral imperative remains but it is a solipsistic world: what is to be the measure of the 'needful' and 'important'? The very existence of the words is proof of our moral natures: we are value-makers by nature; we cannot live without constantly making judgements and decisions. But neither can we do it on our own. It is a kind of existential nightmare that throws individuals (in this case teachers) on to their intuitive, unsupported resources; that regards tradition and culture as suspect constraints upon the evolution of untrammelled individuality. Of course, in practice there are few teachers whose work would display such a philosophy in so extreme a form but there is no doubt that the general elusiveness of the language here is symptomatic of a debilitating absence of conviction. The strongest discernible commitment is a defensive one: 'to give the child a perspective on institutions which will help him to see himself as maker and participant, rather than victim'. Dixon's infinitely elastic definition of English (p.45) leads to the immensely ambitious proposal that 'the topics for classroom study become in addition the events, language and rituals of school itself and the community'. It leads, too, to a characteristically opaque turn of phrase – a feature that tends to occur when the description of this English teacher touches on the nature of the 'control' he wishes to develop in his pupils: 'the processes the children engage with should enable them to gain insight into and thus control over their own lives'. Any sensible interpretation of this probably stems from the materialistic view of language found in the following extract:

> we must put pupils and teachers in a position to see the way in which language processes their experience of the world and places a grid between

their perception and their interpretation of it. A properly developed reflexiveness would enable the individual, pupil or teacher, to see how he is himself 'made in and through language': and how the society he inhabits, and the culture which informs it, are themselves products of the language which their makers speak.

(Doughty, 1974, p.144)

It is a passage that implicitly accepts that it might be turned against itself: 'a properly developed reflexiveness' must surely prompt us to ask how truthful the metaphor of a grid is, whether the notion of so distinct a separation between our perception and the interpretation that language enables us to place upon it is true to our experience. Are we routinely denied 'control' over our own thoughts and actions because language obstructs our naturally pristine perceptions? Such a way of speaking about language belongs to a philosophy that disallows 'perception' as itself intimately interfused by words, perception that may be variously poor or rich according to the quality of the words of which it is in large part constituted. As a philosophy of language it absolutely contradicts Coleridge's idea of words as 'living powers'.

The idea of perception unsullied by language can be as seductive as the idea of a learner unimpeded by tradition and culture. And as unreal. The metaphor of the grid is quite incompatible with and quite unable to explain the nature and the force of literature. It does not allow for the creative, for that way with words that doesn't come between a 'perception' and our interpretation of it but creates a fresh and original perception that becomes part of our sensibility. We are in this sense 'made in and through language'. This is not, however, what Doughty means. His is a liberationist philosophy in which language figures only as constraint: his 'grid' acts like a prison grille. The consequence of this philosophy (as we have seen) is that it projects teachers and learners into a world without bearings. How are learners to gain the longed for control 'over themselves and the surrounding world'? Materialist philosophies tend to throw up materialist instruments in answer to such questions. Simplified, materialist views of language do the same: in the 1970s we could see emerging that harsh technological idiom which would eventually dominate National Curriculum English. In *Classroom Encounters* we read of the way 'language operates', of the 'strategies' to be used by the teacher in 'his classroom, his own laboratory'. James Britton spoke of 'Our world representation' as 'a storehouse of the data of our experience', of language as 'an organizing tool', 'our principal means of classifying' (Britton, 1975). Britton himself explores D.W. Harding's useful distinction between language used in 'participant' and 'spectator' roles, but it is the former – 'language to get things done' – that represents the dominant interest of those considering questions of language, culture and learning at this time. Britton's antagonism towards subject-based learning could not easily accommodate the idea of literature as the central, defining element in the teaching of English.

As Britton develops his view in his book *Language and Learning* (1975) language is conceived primarily in its instrumental aspect, as a means of control. His definition of the 'participant' uses of language – 'informing people, instructing people, persuading people, arguing, explaining, planning, setting forth the pros and cons and coming to a conclusion' – anticipate the taxonomies of the Cox Report (*English for Ages 5 to 16*, 1989) and National Curriculum English. As, more startlingly, does Doughty's mechanistic view of writing: 'Competence in the written language is a question of matching what one wants to mean to a linguistic form that, in turn, matches the expectations of the audience for whom one is writing' (Doughty, 1974). There is a delusive, formulaic neatness in this definition. It seems to bring under control what we instinctively feel to be a very complex matter; to offer teachers the basis of a scheme in which identifiable means may be brought to the achievement of unambiguous ends. But, of course, the reality of writing is quite different. Doughty's is a description of the act of writing uninformed either by common experience or by the abundant published testimony of writers themselves. 'Meaning' is not an already determined entity waiting to be married to an existing linguistic form. 'Competence' might here be adequately described as far as it applies, say, to bus timetables or football results. But beyond that? By the same token, audiences are not fixed properties awaiting the delivery of a message whose form and content they already know. Writers aren't that docile: they may guess at the 'expectations' of their audience – and then deliberately attempt to defeat, outrage, challenge or ignore them. Such persuasiveness as Doughty's mechanical model possesses is only at the level of formulaic writing, which is exactly the kind that, when it is not drawing attention to its limitations, English is concerned to avoid. Nevertheless, something remarkably like Doughty's words got into the first National Curriculum Order: 'AT3 Writing: a growing ability to construct and convey meaning in written language matching style to audience and purpose' (DES, 1990).

If we ask how such anomalies have arisen and how, in the discussion of the teaching of English, words can come to be used in so inadequate a way we shall find ourselves conscious of an absence: what should have disciplined the words has been more or less explicitly disavowed. The inverted commas that Torbe and Protherough place around the words 'culture' and 'heritage' are symbolically telling in this respect. In thus distancing themselves from these indispensable words, they undoubtedly echo John Dixon's sceptical and very influential consideration of 'the heritage model' of English in *Growth Through English:*

> in the heritage model the stress was on culture as a *given.* There was a constant temptation to ignore culture as the pupil knows it, a network of attitudes to experience and personal evaluations that he develops in living response to his family and neighbourhood.
>
> (Dixon, 1975, p.3)

What was influential and highly problematic in this was not the implication (with which it is easy to agree) that much bad and lazy practice had sheltered under a token commitment to 'great literature'. It was rather the argument that such literature was powerless to reach readers without a radical change in teachers' understanding of their function – an understanding not of their subject matter but of 'culture as the pupil knows it'. The burden that was to fall on to English teachers' shoulders was immense: since 'what is vital is the interplay between his [the pupil's] personal world and the world of the writer, the teacher of English must acknowledge both sides of the experience, and know both of them intimately if he is to help bring the two into fruitful relationship'.

To know both of these worlds intimately is impossible; the book maybe, the child (which of course really means many individual children) never. But the teacher does possess common sense; he develops an instinct for what is apt, difficult, exotic about a book. To suggest that before he can teach *The Wind in the Willows* or *The Secret Garden, Ash Road* or *Macbeth* he must have an intimate knowledge of his pupils' world (particularly when it is described in terms of family and neighbourhood) is to ignore the familiar power of much literature to tell on the mind in regions the teacher cannot explicitly reach. When we are told that the 'heritage model' 'confirmed' the teacher in 'presenting experience (in fictions) to his pupils, rather than drawing from them their experience (of reality and the self)' we have a strong sense of language having grown vapid through detachment from the sources that should have sustained it. How, to be specific, can we fit Dixon's critical description to the experience described by Ted Walker in his autobiographical *The High Path?* Miss Miles was what we would now call a supply teacher; she occupied one afternoon in Ted Walker's school life:

> I wish I could meet Miss Miles again. I should like to tell her that she taught me more about the entrancing power of words in that quiet lull during the Battle of Britain than any teacher subsequently did (including Robert Graves, at whose feet I sat as an undergraduate when he delivered the Clark Lectures). She related the story of Romulus and Remus with such narrative

and descriptive skills that I was left with the most vivid sense of having been actually suckled by the she-wolf, of having handled every rough block of stone built on the seven hills of Rome, of having not only sharpened the knife and stabbed Remus but also of having been Remus himself, dead by my twin brother's hand.

...She was ice-cool and showed not the slightest interest in us; but she spoke impromptu English prose like an angel. Frequently I am asked by English teachers how best to encourage their pupils to produce better creative writing. 'Do as Miss Miles did,' I say; and I am not thanked for what is considered to be a flippant answer.

(Walker, 1982, pp.54–55)

No 'model' of teaching will ever correspond to what passes between the minds of teacher and pupil. The price of insisting otherwise is to distort the nature and ignore the quality of the kind of experience for which Ted Walker was so grateful:

A heritage model, with its stress on adult literature, turns language into a one-way process: pupils as readers, receivers of the master's voice. How, we may ask, do these private activities of writing and reading relate to the stream of public interaction through language in which we are all involved every day, teachers as much as pupils? The heritage model offers no help in answering, because it neglects the most fundamental aim of language – to promote interaction between people.

(Dixon, 1975, p.6)

The personification of 'heritage model' here obstructs clear thinking. This is an extremely crude account of the relationship between language, culture and readers. We might hesitate to describe Shakespeare, Dickens or Wordsworth as 'promoting interaction between people' but it is surely the case that in reading them we are sharing visions and perceptions which, in so far as they then become active in our own language and perceptions, enter the wider social and public life to which we belong. (This is what Holbrook meant in describing English as developing 'that richness of the individual being which releases sympathy and creative energy in community'.) Dixon writes as if there were no possibility of bridging the gap between 'private activities' and 'public interaction' unless it is planned for and made visible; as though, unless we have evidence that it *has* been bridged, we must conclude that language has been 'a one-way process'. It is obvious (think of Ted Walker's example) that this is a travesty. However, the consequence here is that Dixon arrogates 'interaction between people' above the 'private activities of writing and reading'. His sympathies thus align him with the teacher for whom 'the processes involved while responding [in discussion] to the film' are more important that the value of the film itself.

These processes (which, we remember, were said by Dixon to embrace the 'sum total of the planned and unplanned experiences through language by means of which a child gains control of himself and the surrounding world') are not easily inspected and described. Certainly they are too elusive to be caught in words that might form the basis of a common understanding of what 'English' is. Nonetheless, it was just such an understanding that HMI attempted to formulate in 1984 (DES, 1984). Torbe and Protherough's tone and vocabulary foreshadow the terms in which that attempt would be made, terms creating the strong impression that a wholly new, clearly grasped and publicly accessible version of the subject lay to hand:

> it was an important point of departure from the past when English teachers recognized that language was not one indivisible thing but a complex of activities with four distinct modes: listening, talking, reading and writing. It was an even bigger step to perceive that each mode involved a *spectrum of operations*.
>
> (Torbe and Protherough, 1977, p.12–13)

In the phrase I have italicized are foreshadowed the highly complicated, unmanageable and theoretically dubious taxonomies of the 1990 Order for National Curriculum English. This is a painful irony. What Torbe and Protherough describe as 'an important point of departure' is little more than a commonplace observation. However, in claiming that 'spectrum of operations' as the special business of 'English', they helped to establish the terms in which official definitions of the subject would be couched, definitions that would accomplish the astonishing feat of both rendering English intolerably burdensome and depriving it of its distinctive identity. Listening, talking, reading and writing are universal activities, common to all subjects of the curriculum; the facts of life, so to speak, from which we should *begin* our consideration of what it is that distinguishes separate disciplines. What begins publicly with *English from 5 to 16* (DES, 1984) is an attempt to describe the 'spectrum of operations' in such a way as to suggest that 'English' is specially responsible for those four modes and that, as the phrase suggests, the route to their mastery is a technical one.

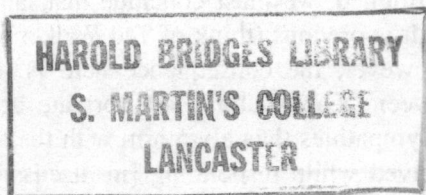

CHAPTER FOUR
Controlling English: Public Accounts

"When *I* use a word", Humpty Dumpty said, in rather a scornful tone, "it means just what I choose it to mean – neither more nor less."
"The question is", said Alice, "whether you *can* make words mean so many different things".
"The question is", said Humpty Dumpty, "which is to be master – that's all."
(Carroll, p.214)

As David Holbrook used the word, 'sensibility' was a unifying concept. In its implication of a union of thought and feeling it was a vital word in any claim for 'English' as a distinctive subject. HMI's *English from 5 to 16: Curriculum Matters 1* (DES, 1984) both espoused the word ('Good English teaching is an education of the intellect and sensibility') and more or less emptied it of meaning. For, as we have seen, in the tradition evoked in Holbrook's use of the word, it embraces 'the inward world with which we first have to deal before we can deal with the outside world'. With *5–16,* on the contrary, the 'outside world' was to be met head on: '...the objectives can best be attained by setting tasks which require communication for real or realistic purposes and in which particular skills need to be used'. 'Communication' and 'real' are the key and much repeated words – key to the values to which *5–16* gives body. The reality of the inner life (a life that doesn't answer to descriptions in terms of 'purpose') is not included in the scope of 'real' as HMI uses the word. The overwhelming emphasis of the document is thus materialist and functional: 'the most effective way of developing language competence is by applying it to an increasing range and variety of real needs and purposes in which something of genuine interest is communicated' (DES, 1984).

Many respondents to *English from 5 to16* accused HMI of temporizing 'with a growing neglect of literature in schools, and of poetry in particular' (DES, 1986). HMI had declared literature to be 'at the heart of the English curriculum...only in literature will pupils encounter language at its most highly wrought, capturing, shaping and combining experience, thought and feeling' (DES, 1984). This is true and well-said, but fatally undermined by the pragmatic vocabulary which surrounds it. Where would teachers of English recognize their subject in the 'aims' for writing?

> to write for a range of purposes;
>
> to organise the content of what is written in ways appropriate to the purposes;
>
> to use styles of writing appropriate to the purposes and intended readership;
>
> to use spelling, punctuation and syntax accurately and with confidence.
>
> (DES, 1984, p.3)

It is the central irony of *English from 5 to 16* that 'English' is simultaneously asked to bear the weight of general responsibility for 'language development' in all its aspects and deprived of that particular focus which the recognition of literature's place at 'the heart of the English curriculum' had appeared to promise. The elasticity prefigured in John Dixon's account of English stretches the subject to the point where its limits seem to be those of the school curriculum itself. Despite the exhaustive definition of 'objectives' and 'purposes' and 'skills', the eventual sense is not of expansion and enrichment but of a narrowing and loss of focus. What is left as distinctively the province of the English teacher appears to be little more than grammatical terminology and 'knowledge about language':

> to teach pupils *about* language, so that they achieve a working knowledge of its structure and of the variety of ways in which meaning is made, so that they can use it with greater awareness, and because it is interesting.
>
> (DES, 1984, p.3)

In a document dedicated to establishing the priority of 'real and realistic purposes' in English this is a strangely evasive statement. Could there be nothing sharper, more 'realistic' and useful indeed, to say about the value of such 'knowledge' than that it is 'interesting'? It hardly smacks of firm purpose and conviction. How would this new form of knowledge, this teaching 'about' language, differ from English teachers' present knowledge and practice? What is so striking and (as events would prove) so significant in HMI's papers is that they show so little active, formative consciousness that, in so far as the teaching of English has been rooted in the study of literature and has thereby encouraged the imaginative uses of language, it has drawn upon a philosophy extensively documented within its own tradition. In calling for an inquiry to establish what children should 'know about how the English language works' HMI discountenanced the fundamental tenet of that philosophy: that the growth of the capacity to use and understand the native language is, as the metaphor conveys, an organic process which English teachers are there to encourage, *par excellence,* in its imaginative dimension. The new metaphors were mechanical ones:

> a pre-requisite to a national policy statement about the teaching of English is agreement about what our children should be taught about the English language and how it works. Such agreement is necessary if they are to grow up to be informed, effective and sensitive users of our language: in control of it rather than at its mercy and open to manipulation by those who use language to persuade and confuse. Without such agreement and without some generally agreed ways to talk about the workings of language, we are not in a position to determine what our teachers need to know or how to set about teaching it to them.

(DES, 1986, Foreword)

Effectively, this severs 'English' from its past and renders its previous achievements null, since 'informed, effective and sensitive users of our language' can only emerge following agreements the profession has still to reach! HMI's metaphors are the direct legacy of the Bullock Report (DES, 1975). Bullock had called for teachers to be given 'an explicit understanding of the operation of language' so that they might 'control the growth of competence' in their pupils. For Newbolt the 'control of the instrument which shapes our thought' had been essentially an art and would develop in our reading of English literature through 'the discovery of ourselves in our native environment'. For Bullock and HMI the control is something we exercise *over* that environment. To the most euphoric exponents of this idea in the eighties (like the linguist I referred to in chapter 2), the prospects were Faustian. We would recognize 'mature, educated native speakers', by their 'ability to exercise *full* [my italics] control over their native environment by their language behaviour' (Carter and Burton, 1982).

If automata could think, that is how they might see themselves. The interest of the statement is not in its truth (it is quite false) but in its representativeness. It condenses not only the conception of language that informs *English from 5 to 16* but also the essence of the generic vocabularies that were to dominate the centralizing curriculum documents of the 1980s. That these vocabularies were generic is no surprise. A centralizing movement, particularly when it arises from an effort to control and standardize a variety of individual philosophies and activities (in this case the subjects of the curriculum), will tend to stress what they have in common rather than what sets them apart. There will thus tend to be a tension between the generic vocabularies and those reflecting the values and traditions of particular subjects. The problem with 'English' at this time was that if HMI felt such a tension it nonetheless capitulated to the utilitarian idiom then establishing itself. The constant insistence that language should be used for 'real or realistic purposes' aligned HMI with the overwhelmingly utilitarian and vocational emphasis of the government's 1987 consultation document on the National Curriculum:

> The subject working groups [for the National Curriculum] will be expected to ensure that the content and teaching of their subject brings out its relevance and links with pupils' own experience and practical applications; and that the programmes of work contribute to the development in young people of personal qualities and competence, such as self-reliance, self-discipline, an enterprising approach and the ability to solve practical real-world problems, which will stand them in good stead in later life.
>
> (DES, 1987, p.5)

Of course, in one sense it is reasonable to ask that each subject justify itself in relation to its 'continuing value to adult and working life'. The implication, however, is unmistakable: such a justification has not previously been forthcoming and must now be made in terms acceptable to 'the real world'. Those terms (the generic language) implicitly devalue and deny the connection between 'the inward world with which we must first learn to deal' and the 'outside world' (Holbrook, 1961).

The principal feature of the generic vocabularies that unite *English from 5 to 16* and the National Curriculum consultation document is that they both narrow the range of purposes education should serve and oversimplify the relationship between means and ends. The focus on 'the real world' encourages an exaggerated belief that it is to 'the outside world' and its values that we should look for guidance. The conception of education shaping the work of the National Curriculum subject groups as they formulated 'programmes of study...relevant to today's needs' was (as the phrase indicates) dominated by the metaphors of the market-place. In the public language which the 1987 consultation document helped to entrench, education was becoming a commodity to be 'delivered' to the 'consumers'; it was subject, under the surveillance of those 'expert' in 'assessment strategies', to the 'quality control' of 'nationally prescribed testing'. Matthew Arnold said of the English that they are 'so immersed in practical life, so accustomed to take all their notions from this life and its processes that they are apt to think that truth and culture themselves can be reached by the processes of this life' (Trilling, 1956). Metaphors drawn from the market-place and technology possess a seductive power natural to 'processes' that are central to *our* 'practical lives'. Their plausibility makes them dangerous allies when we trust them to illuminate experiences beyond their powers. They are at their most dangerous when they are so deeply embedded in conventional ways of thinking that we forget that they *are* metaphors. The key terms of the Kingman Committee's brief for its *Inquiry into the Teaching of English Language* exemplify this kind of metaphorical plausibility. The committee was 'to recommend a model of the English language...which would serve as the basis of how teachers are trained to understand how the English language works'; additionally, it was 'to recommend what, in general terms, pupils need to know about how language works and in consequence what they should have been taught, and be expected to understand, on this score, at ages 7, 11 and 16' (DES, 1988).

In the event, the significance of the Kingman Report was to lie not in the details of its 'model' (now largely forgotten) but in the impetus its mechanical metaphors gave to the idea of 'knowledge about language' as an instrument in furthering the ends of 'English'. One member of the committee (in a 'note of reservation') doubted that the committee had a clear idea of what those ends were. (Ends are not built into mechanisms and Kingman's terms were entirely mechanical.) The report

> does not come to grips with the central question of how knowledge about language can be shown to be relevant to the educational aims of English as a school subject. Indeed, what these educational aims should be, what English is on the curriculum *for,* is not really explored here with any rigour...
> (DES, 1988, p.77)

Ironically, there is within the pages of Kingman a stimulus to exploring 'what English is on the curriculum *for*'; but it is left to readers to do the work for themselves. The ranging of the various historical versions of the Anglican Burial Service against one another for comment and comparison (in the discussion of reading) might seem to exemplify a mode of language study that is distinctively the province of 'English': a mode based on the conviction that to develop in English is to develop in power of judgement. This is not, however, the light in which Kingman encourages us to see them. 'A student of language', it is said, will find much that is fascinating in juxtapositions such as this:

> So also is the resurrection of the dead. It is sown in corruption: it is raised in incorruption; it is sown in dishonour; it is raised in glory: it is sown in weakness; it is raised in power: it is sown a natural body; it is raised a spiritual body...And so it is written, The first man Adam was made a living soul; the last Adam was made a quickening spirit...The first man is of the earth, earthy: the second man is the Lord from heaven.
> (From the *Book of Common Prayer,* 1662)

> So it is with the resurrection of the dead. What is sown in the earth as a perishable thing is raised imperishable. Sown in humiliation, it is raised in

glory; sown in weakness, it is raised in power; sown as an animal body, it is raised as a spiritual body.

If there is such a thing as an animal body, there is also a spiritual body. It is in this sense that the Scripture says, 'The first man, Adam, became an animate being', whereas the last Adam has become a life-giving spirit. The first man was made 'of dust of the earth': the second man is from heaven.

(From the *New English Bible*, 1970)

(DES, 1988, p.40)

In considering the changes in cadence, idiom and vocabulary that are to be observed as one looks across these and other versions, one is aware of being much more than 'a student of language'. Estimating the significance of these changes is a matter of judgement, in this case judgement that will arise out of a sense of the adequacy of the language to its tremendous subject. If we wish to argue, for instance, that the substitution of 'a perishable thing' for 'in corruption' enfeebles and trivializes the 1662 version, we shall be calling upon much more than anything the committee means when it uses the phrase 'knowledge about language'. There are no linguistic criteria by which we can arrive at our judgement and advance our argument that in the word 'perishable' the modern translators have shed a wealth of moral and metaphysical meaning; that the result calls up the world of market-gardening and commodity shelf-life rather than the tremendous ideas of original sin and resurrection.

Any English teacher who appreciates the point of that 'collation of the present with the past' knows that in observing changes in language we are tracking changes in sensibility and culture and that these are matters of continuous moral and spiritual importance. He is thereby well-placed to understand the distinctive contribution that his subject should be making to children's education – to know 'what English is on the curriculum *for*'. If 'the culture...has to be revitalised by each generation', then English teaching conceived and practised in the light of such an understanding has a noble contribution to make.

If we are capable of making the necessary observations and discriminations amongst those passages from the Anglican Burial Service (as in other passages of prose and verse quoted by the committee) it will be as a result of broad and considered reading, of a developed habit of attention to words, their combinations and their intrinsic relations with our experience of the world. Intermittently the Kingman Committee seems to turn its back on the mechanistic terms of its brief and to acknowledge this: 'Children who read Tolkien and then write their own fairy stories are engaged in a total process of language development which, among other advantages, may one day contribute to the writing of clear, persuasive reports about commerce or science'. This is perhaps the most important sentence in the entire report. The committee seems to accept that literature must be central to the kind of study of language that marks off English from the rest of the curriculum ('What is English *for*?'). What the committee acknowledges in that sentence is the primacy not of models or systems of any kind but of culture, of a guided immersion in the best the language has to offer for the age at which the child approaches it.

The keynote in Kingman is, however, quite different: 'it is just as important to teach about our language environment as about our physical environment, or about the structure of English as about the structure of the atom'. The disconnection from the 'environment' of Newbolt – which, it will be recalled, united the inner and the outer – is complete. The formative metaphors of the Kingman Report, composed as they are from the familiar technological lexicon, are not examined for their accuracy or their value. Brought to bear on the passages quoted ('rich mines for literary and linguistic working') the tools of linguistic analysis yield embarrassingly modest results: a 'student of language' would note 'varieties of spelling in the earlier texts' and that 'sentence breaks are not always marked by full-stops'. English thus descends into triviality, which in this case was soon to be reflected in classroom materials. Under the guidance of a teacher with a feeling for the Gospels as spiritual history and symbolism, it is just conceivable that Key Stage 3 pupils might profit from 'exploring language change' through comparing extracts of four or five lines from the Jerusalem Bible (1966), the Authorized Version (1611), the Wycliffe Bible (1382) and the West Saxon Gospels (1000) (Taylor, 1993). However, a teacher who sees in those passages no more than evidence of 'change in the language environment' will be as incapable as the coursebook writer to convey to his pupils *why* they should bother to track changes in 'spelling', 'word order' and 'word endings'. 'Which do you prefer?' asks the coursebook. If preference is anything but caprice it has to be arrived at through guided judgement – of the necessity for which the coursebook writer gives no inkling.

Kingman (as this example indicates) weakened the idea of the teacher as a judge of language, as someone in whom we should hope to find a sensibility equal to what the committee acknowledges as 'the powerful and splendid history of the best that has been thought and said in our language'. The words directly echo Matthew Arnold's well-known phrases. For Kingman, however, they have ceased to be formative. It is not '*our* language' but *language* that is Kingman's real concern. Very much in the vein of HMI (which recommended teaching pupils 'about language...because it is interesting'), but much more expansively, Kingman wanted children to make 'systematic comparisons with other languages learned or used in school and in present day British society, so that an interest in linguistic diversity might be encouraged'. The principal objection is not that this is impracticable (how could there be time for an engagement with that 'splendid history' and for the ambitious linguistic programme suggested?) but that an interest in language – 'linguistic diversity' – is a hollow thing without a prior or accompanying understanding of what *a* language is. Such an understanding can only come from as thoroughgoing an experience as possible of the culture of one's native language. That indeed is an 'entitlement'. Kingman's recommendations made it less rather than more likely that children would receive it. Rather than its detailed model of language it was the note of moralizing intent ('the duty of all teachers to instil in their pupils a civilized respect for other languages') that was to be of key significance in the teaching of the subject. In amplifying that note and substantiating Kingman's commitment to linguistic diversity, the Cox Report (DES, 1989) would propel 'English' into areas it had never previously inhabited.

The Kingman Report was 'produced within a very tight deadline' (DES, 1988). Soon afterwards the Cox Committee also found itself obliged to 'work at a hectic pace' (Cox, 1991). The resultant note of nervousness in its report was understandable: 'some changes will almost certainly prove necessary in the light of experience'; 'great importance' was 'attached to flexibility in arrangements for revision'. The nervousness notwithstanding, the committee felt it had produced a version of English suitable for adoption in the National Curriculum. It had its firm beliefs:

> While we firmly believe that the best practice reflects a consensus rather than extreme positions, it is important that this is not seen as some timid compromise but rather as an attempt to show the relation between these different views within a larger framework.

> (DES, 1989, chapter 2.6)

This is the language of a committee working at uncomfortable speed on an impossible task: 'best practice' is very unlikely to result from consensus and, logically, can never arise from extreme positions. If we judge a position to be 'extreme', we are implying that it is a position from which no good can be expected. However, one person's 'extreme position' is another's articulate conviction. According to Cox, 'an unfortunate feature of much discussion of English has been the false and unhelpful polarization of views'; for instance, 'people set in opposition...utilitarian and imaginative aims'. But that is not a 'false polarization'; 'utilitarian' and 'imaginative' *are* opposites. The standard meanings of the words make it impossible to embrace both. A conviction that either is to be preferred has to be argued for; we have to make judgements. We can agree that Cox's English and the resultant 1990 National Curriculum Order for English encompassed and highlighted much good practice and, to that extent, gave something of a useful focus to the work of less confident teachers. However, no consensus will automatically command allegiance. Being itself the outcome of judgements – sound or unsound – it calls for judgement itself.

That the committee was not sure of itself or of the values embraced by the consensus it claimed to have reached is clear from the manner of its appeal: its appeal is not to the internal coherence of the argument but to the reader to look upon the consensus in a favourable light – it should not be 'seen as a timid compromise'. This is an emotional, not an intellectual appeal. What the committee expresses may be a 'belief' but it hardly sounds firm. And for good reasons. Cox was not at liberty to found its beliefs in anything firmer than the framework by which it was constrained. Consensus had to be reached within terms that were not of the committee's choosing. It had no choice but to seek 'compromise'. Whatever the convictions of its individual members, the obligation to produce a version of English which, in its structure and forms of assessment, would be identical to those of all other subjects of the National Curriculum, made 'compromise' inevitable.

With Cox, as with Kingman, one is conscious of contradiction and disunity within the very language of the report itself. Cox reflects contradictory ways of thinking about language (a *real* 'polarization of views') that make consensus impossible. There are points where, in drawing upon the inherited language of moral conviction, the report acknowledges the principles that should inform the definition and practice of the subject and supplies a standard by which we may judge its own recommendations. Through literature, teachers should 'promote a sense of excitement in the power and potential of language'; 'experiments in language are not only acceptable but to be encouraged' and children should have sufficient confidence to allow their own personal 'voice' to imbue their writing' (DES, 1989). 'Excitement', 'experimental', 'personal': the words are not easily reconciled with the 'attainment target' for writing: 'to construct and convey meaning in written language, matching style to audience and purpose'. This is a formulation suitable for describing the 'targets' of the advertising and public relations industries. That is, it is mechanical; we can achieve such a 'matching style' through bad writing as readily as in good. Turn the light of such a formulation on the report itself and its limitations are obvious. However close a match the committee may have achieved between the style of *its* report and the purpose the report serves, that match is no guide at all to the quality of thought and feeling to be found within it. The 'best writing' demands a subtler, more human description.

In a felicitous moment the committee accepts as much. 'The best writing' is 'vigorous, committed, honest and interesting'. Many teachers of English took against Cox's failure to include the qualities of vigour, commitment and honesty in the statements of attainment in writing (NCC, 1989). Cox had excluded them on the grounds that 'they cannot be mapped onto levels'. Indeed they cannot: and the very notion of precisely differentiated levels of achievement is thereby rendered null. And yet the crux of the matter, the disabling factor, was that Cox had no choice. The committee's given (not freely formed) 'purpose' was to think about English within a framework totally at odds with the spirit and the best practice of the subject. It is only possible to think within that framework (with its ten levels of attainment for each of the three components of Speaking and Listening, Reading, and Writing) by persuading oneself that English is other than it is. To contemplate those abstract words – 'vigour', 'commitment' and 'honesty' – is to realize that, whilst full of meaning to speakers, writers and readers, they nonetheless resist sharp definition. We know when we are in their presence. Often we know it intuitively. This is knowledge for which standard frameworks of the kind Cox was obliged to work with cannot find room. The temptation – the inevitable consequence, one might say – is to deny the reality of such knowledge; to accept, instead, the philosophy implicit in the framework: that what matters, what must be taught and assessed, is what may be objectively set forth. But with English there is much that *cannot* be so set forth.

We here touch upon the central difficulty neither Cox nor the 1990 Order (to all intents and purposes the same: the NCC (1989) espoused most of the practices commended by Cox and all its principles) could possibly resolve: that the requisite objectivity could only be achieved through a drastic distortion of the very values one might have looked to a national committee to protect. That the Education Secretary wished to see the attainment targets and programmes of study printed first in the report was clearly not what the committee had intended (Cox, 1991). There was, nevertheless, a strong logic to that insistence. The obligations of assessment and reporting made it inevitable that teachers would regard the statements of attainment as the point where the values of Cox's English were unambiguously crystallized.

It is in the Cox Report and the 1990 Order that we find the extended and elaborate description of that 'spectrum of operations' involved in each of the 'modes' of listening and talking, reading and writing (Torbe and Protherough, 1977). The Cox Committee, it is true, acknowledged 'problems in defining a linear sequence of language development' and claimed to have 'taken to heart TGAT's comment that "the assessment process itself should not determine what it is to be taught and learned...it should be an integral part of the educational process"'. However, it was the 'assessment process' rather than the larger ends the process should have served that shaped the content and the language of the report. The prevailing technical phraseology invites us to think about language as an object, a form of observable behaviour, open to the kind of precise description at which, constrained by the common framework of assessment, the Cox Committee aimed. (Hence, eventually, the assessment grids and tyrannical tick lists – so scandalously expensive of teachers' time and spirit – that the Dearing Report would attempt to discourage.) Thus the dynamic, elusive actualities of the spoken word are reduced to six sets of 'oral skills'; together constituting the capacity (as with 'Writing') for 'matching style and response to audience and purpose'. The jargon ('Oracy involves teaching and assessing children's language behaviour with other people') delivers 'English' into the world of the hard sell and 'presentational' politics. Level 10 attainers would prove able to 'express a point of view on complex subjects cogently and with clarity, applying and interpreting a range of presentational strategies and assessing their own effectiveness accurately' (DES, 1989). Who would guess from level 10 what every English teacher knows: that 'complex subjects' tend to produce complex reactions, reactions in which passion, prejudice and puzzlement are an inevitable and acceptable part of the movement towards 'cogency' and 'clarity'? Hearts and minds that are honestly engaged in such subjects (say the morality of abortion, the problems of an ageing population or the pollution of the planet) cannot and certainly should not be expected to assess the 'effectiveness' of their 'presentational strategies'. In a pamphlet approvingly quoted by Cox, HMI commended poetry as a 'vital resource of language', a check on words that have become 'separated from moral and emotional life...a deadening trail of clichés which neither communicates with nor quickens the mind of the reader' (HMSO, 1987). The jargon of oracy has here become 'separated from moral and emotional life', that vital resource rendered inert.

That 'vital resource' was indeed a relatively weak element in the Cox consensus. Rather than accepting the traditional view of literature as formative of the moral and emotional life (exercising, intangibly, its own disciplines upon thinking, feeling, speaking and writing) the Cox Committee placed its faith in the morally neutral concept of 'knowledge about language'. It was nonetheless assumed that moral effects would follow. 'The world would be a better place if people were able to talk coherently about the many language problems which arise in contemporary society'. What children needed to 'know about language' was 'its uses in literature, language variation, bilingualism, language change, ambiguities and problems in communication, the writing system, etc...The data are all around: facts and figures about language in Britain and around the world' (DES, 1989). Such studies would help children to develop 'a firmly based but flexible and developing linguistic identity' in our 'multi-cultural, multi-lingual society'.

The excited rhetoric of internationalism and multi-culturalism (as the social ambitions grow more expansive so the language becomes more vapid) is in sharp contrast to the modest role assigned to the 'heritage of [English] literature'. It is one way in which 'messages are conveyed'. This is the language of consensus at its weakest, all conviction spent. The absence of direction on what British children should read (Shakespeare excepted) is thus to be expected. It is literature in its supposed instrumental function, its 'role' as a mediator of overt or implicit messages that receives the most emphasis. Teachers are to ensure that 'reading literature for enjoyment and responding to it critically' includes (as 'part of the equal opportunities policy across the curriculum') the 'fact' that 'there are authors who have not traditionally formed part of the literary "canon" in the past'. The chosen books must 'encompass a balanced range of presentations of other societies and of ethnic and social groupings and life-styles within our own society'. The object is not so much steady engagement with the literature and culture of the native language as the inculcation of tolerant attitudes towards a variety of cultures. The being envisaged in that 'flexible and developing linguistic and cultural identity' is thus not the deeply cultured polymath who might make sense of the phrase. That identity belongs to a set of attitudes which it is the responsibility of teachers to induce.

Consensus tends – and is usually intended – to placate people; to draw the sting from the disparate convictions it embraces. What consensus never does is to inspire. For that to happen conviction is necessary. This makes the whole 'knowledge about language' episode very instructive. For, as Cox's Utopian rhetoric indicates, what had begun life as an instrumental concept ('the workings of language') soon took on the contours of a vision. Why has the vision faded? There are traces of it in the 1995 Order but the rhetoric is dead. The reasons are only partly political (the government's refusal to allow publication of materials from the LINC – 'Language in the National Curriculum' – Project). As a constituent of English, 'knowledge about language' was fatally flawed: no one was prepared to make a case for its value in developing children's command of English. The consensus united a degree of coyness and a kind of agnostic aestheticism very surprising in relation to knowledge of any sort. Sir John Kingman had rather lamely said that 'there is no positive advantage in ignorance' (DES, 1988). To the National Association of Advisers in English, as to NATE, 'knowledge about language' didn't 'need to be justified by claiming it will improve language performance'; it was 'worthy and valuable in its own right', 'intrinsically interesting and socially useful' (Jones and West, 1988). The National Curriculum Council advised that 'the appropriateness and validity of this strand' be 'regularly reviewed' (NCC, 1989) and, despite the absence of conviction implied in its phrases, called for 'substantial in-service training'. That came in the form of LINC, which would 'boost the confidence' of teachers 'who remain insecure about their ability to deliver this strand of the curriculum effectively' (Carter, 1991).

Unfortunately the director of LINC seemed as puzzled – or as unwilling to commit himself – as anyone else:

> A major unanswered and unexplained question in knowledge about language for pupils concerns the relationship between knowledge about or reflection on language and a development of competence in the use of language. Such a connection is plausible, but in the absence of evidence of the kind required by extensive longitudinal studies, it cannot be demonstrated. What can be said is that pupils are likely to benefit from detailed consideration being given to the forms and functions of language variation. Such is the importance of an ability to control language in all its many variations that the more angles that can be provided on those variations the better.
>
> (Carter, 1991, p.16)

This is where Kingman's 'control of the language environment' leads – into uncertainty and contradiction. Is there really no way short of 'extensive longitudinal studies' by which we could judge the value, the success or failure of 'knowledge about language'? Of what use are those 'angles' on 'language variation' if they cannot be shown to develop 'competence in the use of language'? No answer is possible within the terms used. In deciding whether our use of language is improved by such knowledge we have to make judgements. 'Competence' (as the word is used here) does not include judgement. Competence lies in the 'control' of 'language varieties' as an end in itself. This is an inadequate idea: there are some varieties we should *not* want to control; and we can only know what these are by using our judgement. The LINC director's own prose exhibits one such variety: 'It should be a universal educational goal to empower pupils to...deploy and reflect on the deployment of as wide a range of language varieties as possible'. Even, it follows, the 'variety' exemplified in that very sentence. But no, to *reflect* on that 'variety' is to see why it should not have been used in a discussion of English. For the metaphor of 'deployment' derives from that dehumanizing technological-military idiom that 'English' should vigorously challenge rather than collude with.

That, of course, is a judgement. It is not of the kind that will be developed by the sociolinguistics which – echoing the more outlandish prescriptions of the 1990 Order – LINC outlined for *children*: 'differences and distinctions between societies with predominantly literate or oral cultures; the power of the spoken language in the history of language change' etc. (Carter, 1990). Lacking a philosophy of language, a shaping sense of values and of culture, LINC was largely indifferent to questions of judgement, of moral and aesthetic choice. One of the consequences is the simultaneous expansion and impoverishment of the English teacher's province. To a working party of teachers devising 'knowledge about language' work for Key Stage 3 'imaginative literature...is an area that is almost overwhelmingly rich in resources and data'. An inauspicious way of describing the heart of English, one might think. And indeed this is a version of English in a state of heart failure:

Reading

1. Collecting codes, signs and signal systems (an introduction to semiotics).

Reading is interpreted here as reading media texts and the world at large as well as printed texts.

(Carter, 1990, p.95)

Reading 'the world at large' plunges English into farce. It means 'reading uniforms, sport strips, T-shirts, fashion, personal objects'. Learning about 'language forms and functions' can be precipitated by asking 'a class to empty its bags and pockets'. This is called 'collection of data'. The anticipated profusion of 'texts may vary from bus tickets to *David Copperfield*'. Contrary to Sir John Kingman's view that there is 'no positive advantage in ignorance', without a sense of relevance (which is itself dependent upon a sense of relative value) knowledge may be distracting and destructive. At Key Stage 3 LINC recommended the study of sports strips *and* 'how grammar grows in young children', of bus tickets *and* 'the syntax and pragmatic effects of modal verbs' (Carter, 1990).

Such work, it was claimed, was a matter of 'redressing the balance between the privileged status of literature and the Cinderella status of language'. Status of course is not the same as value. It seems unlikely that an interest in English that confines itself to providing 'angles on language variation' can have much to say about literature and about the value of

'English' itself. Do teachers and pupils need the 'metalanguage' offered in order to 'talk about language more precisely and economically'? (It is important to be clear on this. It is quite conceivable that, come the next revision of National Curriculum English, there will be those who wish to restore 'knowledge about language' to the 'status' it had in the 1990 Order.) In practice, the 'metalanguage' too easily becomes a tool of that 'objective intelligence' which, confining itself to 'what is no more than a narrow mode of perception' (Hughes, 1994), both mistakes its object and leaves it poorer than it found it:

> The car ploughed uphill through the long squalid straggle of Tevershall, the blackened brick dwellings, the black slate roofs glistening their sharp edges, the mud black with coaldust, the pavements wet and black. It was as if dismalness had soaked through and through everything. The utter negation of natural beauty, the utter negation of the gladness of life, the utter absence of the instinct for shapely beauty which every bird and beast has, the utter death of the human intuitive faculty was appalling. The stacks of soap in the grocers' shops, the rhubarb and lemons in the greengrocers! the awful hats in the milliners! all went by ugly, ugly, ugly, followed by the plaster-and-gilt horror of the cinema with its wet picture announcements, 'A Woman's Love!', and the new big primitive chapel, primitive enough in its stark brick and big panes of greenish and raspberry glass in the window. The Wesleyan chapel, higher up, was of blackened brick and stood behind iron railings and blackened shrubs. The Congregational chapel, which thought itself superior, was built of rusticated sandstone and had a steeple, but not a very high one. Just beyond were the new school buildings, expensive pink brick, and gravelled playground inside iron railings, all very imposing, and mixing the suggestion of a chapel and a prison.
>
> (D.H. Lawrence, 1960, p.157)

Quoting this passage, the director of LINC claims that

> the role of grammar here is to provide analytical categories not for their own sake but in support of *making intuitions more precise*. With a knowledge of noun–phrase organisation in English the teacher and students can, if required, penetrate further into the text and in the process *make their literary insights both more accountable as well as more retrievable for others*. [my italics]
>
> (Carter, 1990, p.115)

The 'metalanguage' threatens to dispossess readers of their already existing and perfectly adequate intuitive knowledge; indeed the passage from *Lady Chatterley's Lover* relies for its force upon that 'living intuitive faculty' which Lawrence finds denied in the scene he describes. The potency of the writing lies in Lawrence's ability to harness the power of the common language to express his intuitions. The language, so to speak, meets him half-way. 'Black' and its variants are words of deep moral and emotional resonance in the vocabulary of English. Its 'different grammatical categories' are abstractions of no importance in the way English speakers will naturally respond to such words, which have a longer, deeper and more significant history than the abstract phrases referring to them. The same may be said of words like 'beauty', 'death' and 'gladness'. It is their very rootedness, their unquestionable significance in our developed sense of relative worth, that Lawrence invokes in describing a scene that seems to symbolize a decayed civilization.

Lawrence's strength is to produce an image of negation, to draw upon the metaphysical and rhythmic potency of the English language to make us *feel* the absence of beauty, to shape a sense of loss. The syntax expresses both the exhaustion of the town and the exasperation it provokes. As English speakers we know where we are with writing of this kind; it works within the common language. The phrases italicized in the prose of the LINC director do not. It is not simply that it is difficult to know what 'a literary insight' would be or how we will recognize that an 'intuition' has become 'more precise'. What makes the promise a hollow one is that it is here expressed through a vocabulary borrowed from irrelevant metaphorical fields: 'accountable' and 'retrievable' belong respectively, I suppose, to the fields of management and computing. Lawrence's metaphors advance his meaning; 'accountable' and 'retrievable' obscure, even deny, a natural process. We cannot say precisely what they mean but we can see that they are trying to tell us that we cannot talk about the common language unless we command a metalanguage to do it with. That is alienating and false. If we are reading the passage with the quality of attention it demands we don't in any case find ourselves wanting to 'talk about language' in this way. We want to talk about *what* is being said. And when we are inevitably drawn into talking about *how* it is said (we may sense an overbalance of Lawrence's exasperated disgust), it is not knowledge of noun–phrase organization that will enable us to 'penetrate further into the text'.

To the extent that this false sophistication has gained a hold in recent years, it has weakened understanding of what teachers will need as they approach the 'major works of literature' they must now study with their pupils at Key Stages 3 and 4. Objective forms of 'knowledge about language' are of scant value. The 'history of language change and variation', for instance, is a subject for academic linguists: the *imaginative experience* of that history is what we should as a matter of course be concerned with in 'English'. This is not a matter of getting children to 'identify some of the major changes in English grammar over the centuries' (DES, 1990); or of 'considering the development of

English...how usage, words and meanings change over time' (DFE, 1995). Children aren't going to 'learn about how the English language developed' through simply picking out 'words or expressions...that seem "old" or "unusual"' in John Evelyn's arresting description of the Great Fire of London (Seely and Kitchen, 1995). This is to maintain the error of rating abstract knowledge above the cumulative awareness which should become part of educated sensibility. Time spent on such work (or on the kind of ill-focused 'explorations of language change' I discussed earlier) is time unavailable for the development of that awareness. A study of the development of English that confines itself to identifying changes in spelling, vocabulary and grammar is like a history of mankind that confines itself to a description of anatomy. Our understanding of language and history alike is feeble unless we accept that the roots of both are moral and spiritual. We do not need the gospel of St Matthew in order to show this. Any work of literature, whether written for children or adults, will answer. To read, say, *Othello, Mansfield Park* and *The Rainbow* with discriminating attention is to be introduced to the history of the English language at a depth with which no abstract examination of syntactical or lexical change can possibly compare. Each of these texts is centrally concerned with relationships between men and women. The language in which these relationships are explored and exhibited, its moral reach and charge, is different in each case. Each, nonetheless, is palpably connected with the others in the unbroken continuity of English and its literature. To read these books is to enter into that history, to know it from the inside. Whilst we are inside that language it is to much more than language that we are attending:

> But there are certainly not so many men of large fortune in the world as there are pretty women to deserve them. Miss Ward, at the end of half a dozen years, found herself obliged to be attached to the Reverend Mr Norris, a friend of her brother-in-law, with scarcely any private fortune, and Miss Frances fared yet worse.
>
> (Jane Austen, 1953, p.21)

Those two sentences *are* a history of a set of moral and mercenary relations in a particular corner of English society at a particular time, and the syntax not only enshrines the spirit of calculation governing those relations but registers the irony of the eye that records it. It is a world away from the English of:

> O my soul's joy,
> If after every tempest come such calm,
> May the winds blow till they have wakened death,
> And let the labouring bark climb hills of seas,

Olympus high, and duck again as low
As hell's from heaven. If it were now to die
'Twere now to die most happy.

(Shakespeare, 1984, p.92)

and of:

At home, even so near as Cossethay, was the vicar who spoke the other magic language, and had the other, finer bearing, both of which she could perceive, but could never attain to. The vicar moved in worlds beyond where her own menfolk existed. Did she not know her own menfolk: fresh, slow, full-built men, masterful enough, but easy, native to the earth, lacking outwardness and range of motion. Whereas the vicar, dark and dry and small beside her husband, had yet a quickness and a range of being that made Brangwen, in his large geniality, seem dull and local.

(D.H. Lawrence, 1958, p.9)

None of these passages could have been written at the same period as either of the others. Language and substance are rooted, commingled, in history. Each nevertheless draws from the traditional language to speak to us of a phase of the spirit, whether of desiccation, of yearning or of uncertain fulfilment. The Shakespearean moment is one in which the realities of Heaven and Hell are as immediate as the ecstasy that prompts Othello's image. The spiritual yearning that possesses the Brangwen women is a much finer thing than drives Jane Austen's embittered Miss Ward into the arms of the Reverend Mr Norris. In moving from *Othello* through *Mansfield Park* to *The Rainbow* we are indisputably experiencing the reality of 'language variation' and change, but we are encountering it through work of a quality that expands our sense of the possibilities of experience and the power of language to record them. Not all children will read literature of this quality; but all need teachers who see why it should be a touchstone for our work in English.

CHAPTER FIVE
Models for Writing

Many years ago, reading Tolstoy's essay on Maupassant, I was struck by his short list of indispensable qualifications for good writing. These were: a perspicuous style (I have to accept the translator's adjective), a moral foundation – that is a strong stand taken on the problem of good and evil – and lastly the faculty of attention. By attending closely, the writer was to breed attentiveness in his readers, replacing the world with *his* world. Single-mindedness and passion are interchangeable here.

(Bellow, 1994, p.xii)

When, a few years ago, I began to read the Italian writer Primo Levi (1919–87), I was struck by the severe simplicity of his style. Here was a writer who did not waste words; who had schooled himself to make every one count; whose prose allowed the reader no wanderings of attention, as Levi's subject had allowed him no wanderings of his own. That subject was the key to the simplicity. Levi was a survivor of Auschwitz. *Se Questo è un Uomo* (*If This is a Man*) (1958) and *La Tregua* (*The Truce*) (1963) are accounts of Levi's imprisonment. The books make no claim to exhaustiveness; they deliberately avoid the documentary detail and density that the subject invites. That documentation we of course have in plenty: the cataloguing of atrocity, the minutiae of evil. Levi's way is different. His concern is to distil the meaning of what he has experienced and observed. He does it through the recollection of incident, of conversation and of thought. The moving power of this recollection lies in the discipline with which he presents it to his readers. The simplicity, one realizes, lies not only in the language but in an attitude towards language itself. The enormity of Auschwitz exceeds the power of language to describe it or to discover its meaning. And yet without that language we cannot even make the effort. With Levi one is simultaneously conscious of his effort to make the words count intensely and of his consciousness that they are inherently incapable of doing the job.

Where did Levi learn to write in that way? We cannot know. It would be facile to answer: in Auschwitz. And yet that must be partly true. We know, reading the books, that this tremendous and ungraspable subject demands great scruple in a writer trying to make sense of it for those who did not experience it. (Indeed, the general impression is that fundamentally he is trying to make sense of it for himself: his 'audience' is almost incidental.) If we are to be persuaded of the truth of his story we must never be given grounds to feel that he is striving for effect. We must never suspect him to be exploiting his terrible subject in order to produce a particular reaction (of horror, of chastening, of awe). That the reader's reaction inevitably includes those feelings is not due to Levi's conscious design upon him but to his success in abstaining from it. We react, it seems, to what Othello calls 'a round unvarnished tale'. The simplicity of style is a moral fact. The tale, for Levi, had to be told again and again. Indeed it could never be finished. He remained a kind of ancient mariner, a man who could never fully emerge from the 'heart of darkness' into which history had delivered him, a writer for whom the epigraph of his last book, *I Sommersi e I Salvati – The Drowned and the Saved* (1987), is thus singularly appropriate:

> Since then, at an uncertain hour,
> That agony returns:
> And till my ghastly tale is told,
> This heart within me burns.
>
> (Coleridge, 'The Rime of the Ancient Mariner')

We cannot mechanically ascribe the spareness and emotional discipline of Levi's prose to precise historical or cultural circumstances (in his training as an industrial chemist he probably developed habits of exact observation that served entirely unforeseen purposes). What we can say is that he was writing *Se Questo e un Uomo* and *La Tregua* at a time of disillusionment and anxiety about language in modern industrialized and bureaucratic societies. It may be for this reason that one feels within his prose the kind of scruple advocated and exemplified in this country by George Orwell. 'What above all is needed', said Orwell, 'is to let the meaning choose the word, and not the other way about. In prose the worst thing one can do with words is surrender to them' (Orwell, 1960). Levi never 'surrenders to words'. His prose offers us a kind of model – not a stylistic but a moral model. Here is good reason for including Levi (his writing survives more than usually well in translation) amongst the 'non-fiction texts' to be read at Key Stages 3 and 4 – though like any good writing Levi's defies classification in the simple terms of 'explanation, argument, reportage, description' etc. (DFE, 1995). Tolstoy's 'indispensable qualifications' take us to the heart of Levi: the problem of good and evil is his very theme and, in the resoluteness of his attention, he writes in a 'perspicuous style' that 'breeds attentiveness in his readers'. We cannot separate his control of language from his control of his subject matter. We cannot examine his technique as an element separate from the expression of his moral sensibility. The scrupulousness of Levi's writing belongs to the kind of sensibility commemorated in Italo Calvino's tribute to their great compatriot, the poet Eugenio Montale: 'the poet of exactitude, of deliberate choice of vocabulary, of terminological precision, used to pin down the uniqueness of an experience' (Calvino, 1987). Each of these writers recognizes that under modern conditions

> Words strain,
> Crack and sometimes break, under the burden,
> Under the tension, slip, slide, perish,
> Decay with imprecision, will not stay in place,
>
> (Eliot, 1959)

Levi, Orwell, Eliot and Calvino are united in the sense they regularly communicate of being embattled, of needing to resist the tendency of language to degenerate into the generalized and abstract, into imprecision and vapidity. They are united in attempting to demonstrate what is at issue through their own example. They accept that there is the closest relation between thinking, feeling and the quality of the words we live with, have at our disposal. They share an attitude to language that has its natural effect on their own style: honest writing is the result of 'attending closely', of 'single-mindedness and passion' (which Bellow says are interchangeable). Obviously there can be no programme for the inculcation of such attitudes and mental activities. They cannot be willed into existence from the outside. No 'clear definition of basic writing skills' (the only means of improvement the NCC could think of in considering a revision of the 1990 Order) will help. Donald Davie's words, echoing Bellow, suggest why:

> Or consider even that expression so beloved of educators and college administrators – *writing skills. Skill* is obviously a more humane word than *technique.* And yet the very plural form, *skills,* belies what most of us know to be the truth of the matter when we consider in all seriousness how good writing comes about. We all either know from our own experience, or else devoutly believe, that good writing, whether in verse or prose, is the product of the total personality concentrated and attentive to what needs to be said. In other words a paragraph of good prose is not assembled from parts like a good automobile engine. It does not come about from the application at one point of a particular skill (say, punctuation) and at another point of quite another skill (say, imagery)...however necessary it may be to analyse the student writer's problem under separate heads, into categories that seem distinct, we ought always if we can to emphasize that ultimately what is

asked of him, and what he should ask of himself, is on the contrary a singularly unified act of attention.

(Greenbaum, 1985, p.274)

That 'act of attention' embraces the intuitive and imaginative powers of the writer, drawing upon energies and awarenesses he may not be entirely conscious of. Davie speaks as a poet as well as a teacher. He speaks with what, amongst writers, is a familiar emphasis. Douglas Dunn, in a recent collection of essays by poets on their 'craft', says that 'instinct and imagination play a part that is virtually impossible to measure and which contribute in a large way to what might look like conscious decisions' (McCully, 1994). It seems reasonable to call this, in the best possible sense of such a phrase, the standard view. It was not the view adopted in the first National Curriculum Order for English. The attractions of this latter view – that writers 'match style to audience and purpose' – aren't difficult to make out. If 'style' can be 'matched' to 'purpose', purposes can be decided upon (by teachers or pupils) and the accuracy of the 'matching' judged according to stated criteria on what constitutes an appropriate style. It seems to make life easier, to offer a standardizing instrument of control. However, no true writer ever speaks of his or her art in that mechanical way. Edgar Allan Poe spoke of 'the elaborate and vacillating crudities of thought...the true purposes seized only at the last moment' and C.H. Sisson confesses to having 'ordinarily no sense of addressing a particular audience'; sometimes 'it is as if poems formed themselves somewhere beyond the poet's control or awareness' (McCully, 1994). If 'English' is to be worthy of its name it has to accommodate such insights. Neither National Curriculum Order does. Unsurprisingly, therefore, the best work done since 1990 has been in the teeth of official prescription. The evidence has sometimes been startling.

The impulse to congratulate the School Examinations and Assessment Council on publicizing the excellent classroom work from which its 1992 booklet *Key Stage 3 Pupils' Work Assessed* had arisen was quickly checked. It may indeed have achieved its stated 'purpose': 'the assessments shown will help teachers and others come to a common understanding of the attainment targets and statements of attainment at different levels'. However, the achievement of such a purpose is not a sufficient end. For it has been at the expense of 'English' itself; the booklet promotes *mis*understanding. It is worth our attention still. For it put into circulation and consolidated an inadequate conception of writing ('writing skills') that has in some degree become common currency in the schools. Moreover, whilst the 1995 Order scrapped the cumbersome machinery of statements of attainment it retained its predecessor's overall conception of writing: the new 'level descriptions', although less complicated and elaborate than the statements of attainment they replace, are philosophically little distinguished from them.

Key Stage 3 Pupils' Work Assessed certainly contains some lively writing. SEAC, however, is not responsible for any of it. If we are looking for writing that maintains a lively connection with its subject matter, writing that displays imaginative penetration, wit and lucidity, we shall find it amongst the samples of the four year 9 pupils whose work is reproduced in the booklet. Here, for instance, are the first three paragraphs of Katherine's 'The Rime of the Ancient Mariner' (the class were 'asked to re-tell the story in their own words, using words and rhythms to recapture some of the atmosphere of the original'):

> The sea was calm and the boat slept. After the heat of the blazing sun the moon brought cool deliverance. I was unable to sleep. The noose around my neck to which the albatross was hung weighed heavily, not only physically but on my conscience. I removed the bird. Its eyes were open and questioning. Why did I do it?
>
> Now, time had misted over the truth and I could not rightly remember. Thinking about it filled me with guilt. I trudged wearily to the helm of the boat. I was truly sorry for what I had done. If I had known the consequences I would not have killed this beautiful creature that brought the sea breeze.
>
> But I could not stand one more day of persecution. I took one last look at the bird, then I threw it over the side of the ship. I waited to hear the bird enter the water, to be lost forever. The silence was deafening. Surely the water wasn't so far? I peered over the side of the ship, only to see my face staring up at me. The bird had vanished.

(SEAC, 1992, p.48)

This is more sensitive, stronger and more compelling than anything in SEAC's commentary. The reason is not that the commentary is necessarily discursive and therefore less appealing. The reason is that in responding to these samples of children's writing the SEAC assessors are not free agents. Given the modesty of their intentions this may seem surprising. All they intend to do is help teachers understand 'the processes they might go through in reaching their judgements and the kind of evidence they might wish to retain'. Judgements of course are what English teachers, through sensibility, experience and training are well qualified to make. However, the 'processes' the assessors go through in reaching *their* conclusions rarely reflect qualifications of that sort. They serve a highly abstract system of assessment that they must endeavour to place in the best possible light. So, instead of allowing the writing they examine to have its effect; instead of registering the presence or absence of liveliness, of authenticity, of imagination, of sharp and truthful observation; instead of seeing it for what it is and allowing judgement to form itself; instead, that is, of following the established way of the English teacher, they bend their efforts to the demonstration of one overriding – and fallacious – principle: that judgement has only to do with whether or not the writing fulfils the requirements of the National Curriculum. They are less concerned that writing should be good than that it should 'give opportunities for assessment against the statements of attainment'. It matters less that writing should be truthful than that the 'tasks' set by the teacher should 'enable various writing skills to be demonstrated'.

This triumph of an inadequate public language at its most formulaic has since been consolidated in the taxonomies of skills that have found their way into those most faithful representatives of the public language: the coursebooks. A 1995 example offers training in 'writing skills', 'skills in descriptive and explanatory writing', 'analytical skills', 'script-writing skills', 'language skills', as well as 'role-playing skills', 'discussion skills' and 'spelling skills' – all set out against the classroom activity to which they relate, so that pupils shall know exactly which 'skills' they are currently developing (Seely and Kitchen, 1995). SEAC shows what it means to think in such terms. Judgement requires a degree of intellectual suppleness, a quality equal to its object. The SEAC assessors do not judge; they measure. For instance, they acknowledge that Katherine's work on 'The Ancient Mariner' shows qualities of control which are usually found at level 7. Indeed her 'assurance' puts her 'on the borderline of level 8'. The paragraphs quoted above are from her final draft; the booklet also reproduces her first draft, and we can see what we would have surmised: that an already accomplished young writer is learning how to shape her writing into something more imaginatively satisfying than her first (in itself impressive) effort. It is hardly surprising that 'Not much has been changed between the two drafts and the "final version" is more a fair copy than a revision'. What is surprising – indeed incredible – is the assessors' conclusion. Transfixed by the statements of attainment they descend into nonsense. Katherine's, we learn, was 'not very sophisticated redrafting'. The concept of 'sophistication' is circumscribed entirely by statements of attainment which in this instance are bogus. Katherine 'recognizes when redrafting and revising are appropriate (level 6)' but she is not, it is alleged, 'fully demonstrating attainment at level 7d'. For level 7d she must 'demonstrate an increased awareness that a first draft may be changed, amended and re-ordered in a variety of ways'. The implication is inescapable: had Katherine's first draft been worse, she would have been judged to have subsequently done better; she would have produced more 'evidence' in the shape of changes, amendments and re-orderings. No wonder HMI reported that 'there remained much uncertainty [amongst teachers] as to what exactly constituted evidence of attainment at a specific level in written work' (HMI, 1992).

Subservience to systems of assessment produces inevitable distortions of judgement and misleading advice. The writers of the SEAC booklet are not impressed by Katherine's 'discursive essay' on 'Bloodsports'. True, it is the most mechanical of the six pieces of her work reproduced there. She sounds bored. This is obvious from her first pedestrian sentence: 'A blood sport is when animals are hunted'. Looking over all six pieces we can be pretty sure that she didn't warm to this particular 'task'. And no wonder if (as appears to have been the case) it was principally a test of 'the ability to look at both sides of the argument and weigh them against each other before coming to a conclusion'. Maybe Katherine saw that as the stultifying routine it is, bearing little relation to the kind of adult writing that commands our attention. What SEAC calls her 'writing skills' are judged to be still 'fairly unsophisticated'; she still uses 'a fairly limited range of grammatical and lexical features'. How should she improve?

> Katherine should be given a variety of tasks to increase her sense of the relationship between writer and reader and should have opportunities to discuss the suitability of different vocabulary and tone to particular contexts. She needs to practise 'impersonal' or discursive skills to gain more skill in persuasive writing and opportunities will need to be provided by her teacher. She might be shown some examples of effective practice in this genre, in order to help her develop her own structures for this sort of writing. Greater complexity of thought will require more complex expression but this should not be allowed to interfere with her capacity for lucid and descriptive writing.
>
> (SEAC, 1992, p.52)

Increasing the 'range of grammatical and lexical features' would not make *that* a good piece of writing. The assessors are fond of recommending that pupils who don't come up to the mark 'against' particular statements should be shown 'models of writing as examples of effective practice'. Well, compare *their* practice with Katherine's. The eye of Katherine's imagination focuses on a reality of feeling and she finds the words and rhythms to embody it. Her piece *means* something. In the above paragraph nothing is in focus and the writing is lame. The key phrases are muddled or elusive. What is this 'sense of relationship between writer and reader' that it can be 'increased' through a 'variety of tasks'? How is that sense to be 'increased' if the object of these tasks is merely to 'enable various writing skills to be demonstrated'? (The only 'relationship' possible within such an idiom is that of operative to taskmaster.) The limitations of this way of thinking about writing are, ironically, shown up in this very paragraph. It is itself 'impersonal' and 'discursive'. But there is no skill we could recommend its authors to train themselves up in so as to make it more 'persuasive'. We shall only be persuaded by clear thinking and it is not clear thinking that leads to the equation of 'complexity of thought' with 'complexity of expression'. By the latter the assessors seem to mean nothing more sophisticated than 'a wider range of grammatical structures'. Katherine's work already displays a capacity for 'lucid and simple descriptive writing' (though not so simple that she has anything to learn from SEAC's 'sophistication'); nothing is more likely to 'interfere' with it than an insistence that the 'way forward' for her lies in the deliberate cultivation of 'a wider range of grammatical and lexical features'. Such comments are culturally ill-formed (the problem persists in the 1995 Order). We do not find the Sermon on the Mount deficient in 'grammatical and lexical features' any more than we feel uncomfortable with the sublime simplicities of Thomas Traherne's *Centuries*. The idiom of each is powerfully in accord with its meaning. Indeed, we must hope that Katherine's promise is not betrayed; that her already strong and confident command of English will grow to include the ability to see that a facility with such 'features' may as easily be the servant of poor as of good expression. A wise teacher will realize that with continued wide reading her writing will almost certainly develop in subtlety and reach.

It is not good writing of any kind that is formative of SEAC's own. It is a rootless and constrained prose reflecting its authors' allegiance not to any freely chosen version of English but simply to the system they are obliged to interpret and administer. With only the soulless, ready-made phrases of the National Curriculum to work with ('the worst thing one can do with words is to surrender to them') they are incapable of doing justice to qualities such as imaginative vivacity, comic invention or sheer whimsy. Here is part of Katherine's 'Blue Peter Holiday to Venus', a letter:

> You may remember that I won this competition for the most interesting thing to be made out a cornflakes packet, two toilet roll holders, some milk bottle tops and as much string and glue as I wanted. (I made a lifesize working model of a Sopwith Pup.)
>
> I travelled to Venus on a supercharged turbo driven double decker bus. One leaves every morning from Neasden at seven minutes past nine. Travelling at the speed of light there are terrific G-forces and you hardly have time to eat your Marcassin A La Girandine (marinated wild boar and chestnuts – the chestnuts get stuck between your teeth, actually) before you arrive at Venusia at seven minutes past nine.
>
> The natives, though short and squat being about two feet high and six feet wide, were friendly enough (except when they were beating you about the knees to attract your attention). Their heads revolve through three hundred

and sixty degrees which is quite handy when they are driving as they have
the motorcar but no highway code!

(SEAC, 1992, p.44)

There is an inventive relish in this; it goes unnoticed in the official
verdict:

> The way language is used in letters and the particular phrases used to
> describe holidays have been well observed in this letter and Katherine might
> be said to have shown 'an awareness of what is appropriate and
> inappropriate language use in written texts'.

(SEAC, 1992, p.44)

This is where the mechanical idea of writing ability as a matter of
'matching style to purpose and audience' comes to rest. There is no such
thing as 'the way language is used in letters' and there is no sense in the
distinction between 'what is appropriate and what is inappropriate
language used in written texts'. (The 1995 Order has somewhat loosened
but has not abolished the tyranny of this trivial conception: 'ideas...are
organized appropriately for the purpose and the reader. Vocabulary
choices are often adventurous and words are used for effect'.) To ask
teachers to concentrate their efforts on perpetuating these misconceptions
and to assess their pupils' awareness of them is to fall in with what Jill
Pirrie has called 'the monstrous industry spawned by the National
Curriculum, keeping teachers and children endlessly busy but not always
engaging them at a serious or profound level' (Pirrie, 1993b). No one
presently teaching English speaks with greater authority in this
connection.

Every so often a book appears that irresistibly concentrates the mind on
the key questions: what do we teach English for? What kind of teachers
do we need if it is to be done well? What kind of literacy should we be
cultivating? With Jill Pirrie there have been two such books: *On Common
Ground: A Programme for Teaching Poetry* (1987) and *Apple Fire: The
Halesworth Middle School Anthology* (1993a). Both books (anthologies
of children's writing) show comprehensively and exhilaratingly what it
means to teach English 'at a serious or profound level'. Either would have
commanded attention at any time. *Apple Fire* particularly – coming as it
did some three years into the first National Curriculum Order and thus
during the period of its revision – has an exemplary force. It affirms the
central importance of the individual teacher and her culture and it affirms
a faith in the 'strength and courage and intelligence, of ordinary children.'
It reflects a trust in literature – in myth, fable, poetry and story – as

essential to the growth of literacy. It is based on a version of English in which the subjectivity of language is axiomatic: the English language is not 'out-there', a repertoire of 'uses' and 'skills'. For Jill Pirrie it is what it was for the authors of the Newbolt Report: 'the element in which we live and work'. We live in that element from the moment we begin to hear English spoken. What made (and makes) *Apple Fire* exemplary is the challenge it offers both to the cumbersome catch-all English of the 1990 Order and to its replacement. Jill Pirrie's English is more sophisticated and simpler than either. In wishing 'to keep at bay...the usual vocabulary in which teaching is discussed', Edward Blishen hints (in an excellent Foreword) at the nature of Jill Pirrie's 'defiant originality' and the ways in which it inevitably sets her at odds with the philosophies that vocabulary enshrines. If we ask why she neither refers to nor draws upon the characteristic phraseology of the National Curriculum in her Introduction we need look no further than the contents of the anthology for an answer.

To teach 'English' is unavoidably to teach cultural history. It is 'English' teachers who must decide what should count most in that history: what should shape their pupils' experience, what should (in Jill Pirrie's phrase) 'provide new perspectives on the ordinary world'. What does not count in her 'English' is 'knowledge about language' as the National Curriculum defines it. There is no place in her philosophy for the objective study of language, for language as 'data', for studies of changing English grammar or the sociolinguistics of vocabulary. For her what counts is literature, 'the forms and symbols of the language within which [children] come to know themselves, and the grammar within which they will make meaning'. The accessibility and creative, releasing power of those forms and symbols is her starting point. She takes her bearings from the example of Emily and Charlotte Brontë ('within whose narrow world so many have been released into a new awareness which transcends time, place and circumstance') as described by Ursula Le Guin:

> From the time they were seven or eight years old, they wrote, and thought, and learned the landscape of their own being and how to describe it. They wrote with the imagination...They wrote from inside, from as deep inside as they could get by using all their strength and courage and intelligence.
>
> (Le Guin, 1989, p.172)

Ursula Le Guin's phrases stress the autonomy of the imagination and the openness to experience that allows it to flourish: '...experience isn't something you go and *get* – it's a gift, and the only pre-requisite for receiving it, is that you be open to it'. Jill Pirrie's achievement lies in her capacity to induce such an openness in her pupils; in Edward Blishen's words, 'she knows how to cause children to be eager'. This is not a technique or a skill that could be written into a National Curriculum document. It is an attitude, a faith, a capacity to make children believe in their own 'strength and courage and intelligence'. It is a matter of following Ted Hughes' advice to teachers (which Jill Pirrie quotes): 'Their words should be not "How to Write" but "How to say what you really mean" – which is part of the search for self-knowledge and, perhaps, in one form or another, grace' (Hughes, 1967).

Ted Hughes' words inevitably raise questions of content and value. The challenge to the teacher is a cultural challenge. For it is only by experiencing a range of perception and quality of insight superior to our own that we come to know what we *can* use language to mean. 'Self-knowledge', as Hughes uses the expression, must embrace the culture ('the forms and symbols of the language') within which the self has its being. For there is surely no self to *be* known (certainly through language) aside from the cultural forms within which it comes to be expressed. The extent to which it can be known is not within our control (hence, presumably, Hughes' reference to 'grace'). The least we can do for the young is to ensure that the culture *we* inherited is made accessible to them.

Thus, no less for Jill Pirrie's pupils than for the Brontës, is 'the landscape of their own being' a given, an undiscovered country awaiting its verbal topographer. Its general contours are already discernible: they are the existing 'forms and symbols' of which, being born to the language, we are the natural inheritors. We come into that 'rightful inheritance' either haphazardly or in the disciplined way reflected in the pages of *Apple Fire*. The poems

> were written by children learning to think, look, and listen within the good company of other writers. It is when children make that essential personal connection within a text that they recognise themselves and grow into the self-knowledge which is dependent on mastery of language.
>
> (Pirrie, 1993a, p.16)

The 'mastery' in question is a world away from:

> AT3 (Writing) does not offer a clear definition of basic writing skills, the grammatical knowledge pupils must master if they are to become effective writers, and the variety of ways in which competence can be developed.
>
> (NCC, 1992, p.9)

This is a familiar fallacy. What is missing is the recognition that permeates Jill Pirrie's work: that to work with the native language, to teach English, is inescapably to move within a moral, spiritual and emotional element; that to separate 'language skills' from the element in which all language has its existence is both false in ambition and abortive in effect. If a hard focus on 'skills' were the sure route to a generally high standard of literacy we should certainly know it by now. That route has been tried often enough. For Jill Pirrie, command of language is synonymous with the articulation of experience; children have to be brought to feel that they need 'English' to help them to say what most matters to them.

Her teaching, then, flows from a settled and passionate belief in the links between literacy and literature: 'poetry, fable, myth and story'. For these are the bedrock of any culture, the repository of its deepest intuitions and forms of awareness, a 'rightful inheritance'. They continue to speak to us because they touch upon our deepest feelings and the need for significance. Children know this intuitively and it is this intuitive awareness upon which Jill Pirrie builds. She knows that, carefully introduced to language that speaks to them (an English that is a richer, more diverse instrument than they can yet know), they will find their own voices. Once that 'essential personal connection' is made the English already in the child's possession will grow in its power to articulate understanding. *Apple Fire* is the evidence. Her achievement lies in helping her pupils to arrive at an essential balance between respect for those maturer voices to which their teacher introduces them and a confidence in their own; and the confidence surely comes when they feel that the rhythms and inflexions of the tongue to which they are born are continuous with those of the writers they encounter. There is nothing at all exotic in this: these are, as Ted Hughes says in the introduction to *On Common Ground*, 'ordinary children' – 'ordinary in the sense that they come from the whole range of backgrounds provided by a country town in Suffolk, and enjoy no specialised milieu of intellectual or literary or artistic sophistication' (Pirrie, 1987). Ted Hughes speaks of their teacher's ability 'to unlock the resource of so many of her pupils', of the 'secret, creative activity of the mind' that often defies the conventional categories which label children 'advantaged' or 'disadvantaged', able and less able. (Jill Pirrie's classes are 'mixed ability'.)

There is a grace and subtlety in the poems produced by Jill Pirrie's pupils, a level of moral understanding that one cannot say is either a reflection of sensibility or of a growing command of English. It is both; the two are synonymous. And such a development is *natural*. The 'robust commonsense' that she finds in her pupils ensures that the 'essential personal connection' has discernible roots in the world they know best. 'Language and environment are inextricably linked', she says. What she seems to do most impressively is to engender a feeling for language as a mode of expression that both reflects the visible world (these are country children) and gives shape to intuition and feeling. The landscape of Jane Weaver's 'The Dream of Persephone' is a recognizable landscape of poppies, butterflies, crows and trees. But this twelve-year-old girl's description is penetrated by the feeling that has been awakened, or intensified, by the myth. The mythological and the ordinary are fused in a way that affirms the continuing power of the story – 'the Persephone myth is one of those stories that must be told again and again'. Her poem is a vision of the earth made new in Persephone's dream, a paradise rooted in the ordinary: 'Slug trails cover a large stone/like a child's first drawing'. It is a world of the imagination – but imagination working on the 'real' world.

> A brook runs through this paradise
> Like a silver ribbon
> Binding it up into reality.

Typically in these poems the 'real world' is not abandoned but taken up and re-interpreted through the imagination. The result is a depth of understanding that could not be arrived at in any other way. ('Persephone, in particular, has enabled children to write of their earth with a passion which is not a whit diminished by the necessary and cool objectivity of their poetic discipline' (Pirrie, 1994).) 'Old Man Cactus' is a fancy, but a truthful one. Joanne Drake's poem pins down the persistence of the species, its doggedness, the reason for its survival:

> For old man cactus is wiser than the trees,
> He learnt long ago to live in the hot yellow deserts
> Where no other plants survive.
> With great cunning he covered his back in cruel spikes –
> No creature could bite him or drink his blood.
> He knew the great heart of the sun
> And the long cold stab of the night.
> But old man cactus survived them all.

For the authors of the proposed revision of National Curriculum English 'figurative language both in verse and prose' was a linguistic category, a discrete entity for objective study and for programmed use: Key Stage 3 and 4 pupils should 'develop their ability to write poetry' through 'their use of alliteration, imagery' (DES, 1993). (In the 1995 Order this had become 'develop their use of poetic devices'.) 'Old Man Cactus' gives the lie to such thinking. The writer here inhabits her subject through a mode of expression which is a mode of understanding. The personification of the cactus is not a 'device', a decorative or whimsical addition to her thinking, it *is* her thinking. Here is a child who has learned 'to inhabit the silence of contemplation, learned to make leaps of imagination' (Pirrie, 1993b). Above all, says Jill Pirrie (with significant emphasis), 'I do not teach environmental awareness. Rather I attempt to inculcate it at the deepest level through poetry, fable, myth and story'. Speaking of Ursula Le Guin's *A Wizard of Earthsea* she says, 'Reading a novel like this teaches more about conservation than any amount of overt preaching' (Pirrie, 1987). 'Old Man Cactus' contains the justification for 'English' as a school subject. It bears out the claim that language and environment are inextricably linked. In 'articulating a sense of kinship with the earth' Joanne is certainly learning about language. But it is not the knowledge that linguists possess. She uses her inherited language, her native English, to interpret her world and our world. She discovers the power language has to enable her to take possession of her own experience. There is a note of exaltation, of wonder and admiration in the last three lines (the monosyllables are perfectly judged) but can we imagine an 'environmental awareness' more rooted, more informed and more realistic? It is important to insist on the realism. Jill Pirrie speaks of her children's 'attitude to the natural world' as 'essentially unsentimental' and of their 'robust commonsense' as 'an essential ingredient of their writing'. Writing of this kind is hard-headed, penetrated by thought, not merely suffused with feeling: 'Old Man Cactus' includes the plant, its significance and the growth of understanding and wisdom in the child who contemplates and evokes them.

The 'sense of kinship with the earth' is an intuitive possession, to be cultivated, made articulate and coherent through the kind of teaching that produced Matthew Booley's 'The Tree and Uncle George':

> The death of Uncle George
> Is woven into the tree's departure.
> The way he used to limp
> Through Henham Woods
> As the rain slowly seeped
> Through his battered raincoat.
> His half bald head
> Covered in a film of water
> That shimmered in the sun
> Like an overglazed pot.
>
> At times the sun
> Shone down on his wrinkled face,
> Lighting the creases
> Like furrows on a field.
> And his worn shoes
> Were the cut-off roots of the stricken tree,
> Wedging him firmly
> To the living earth.

Uncle George is dead but no more than the stricken tree ('But still there stands a four foot stump/Fifteen years after its fiery fall') is he obliterated. How does a thirteen-year-old boy achieve this level of sophistication? A native intuition, an inborn sense of the connection the poem expresses, has found developed form within the literary culture that is the basis of his English teacher's work:

> Poetry especially has the power to enable them to know their creation in the literary sense. This is to transcend easy sentimentality, reverse alienation and return them to the wilderness earth which has been their home for so many millions of years. From this homecoming grows an atavistic sense of recognition and a responsibility for an earth which must be held in trust for each succeeding generation.
>
> (Pirrie, 1993a, p.21)

That 'atavistic sense' is in 'The Tree and Uncle George'. Is this 'environmental education'; is it 'moral education'? The answer is clearly 'yes' in both cases – but not as a result of their teacher having incorporated 'cross-curricular themes' into English. The problem with 'cross-curricular themes' is one of abstraction: they invite the proselytising and ideological approach. For Jill Pirrie these themes are implicit in the forms of knowledge that we mean in speaking of a 'literary culture' and that she has in mind when speaking of children coming into 'their rightful inheritance'.

It is the depth at which they are already absorbing that inheritance that accounts for the startling authority with which these children write. Emma Walkey's 'The Ghost of the Orchard' was 'made possible' (like the other ghost poems in the collection) by a reading of Leon Garfield's short story 'A Grave Misunderstanding'. This was 'simply...a new perspective on the ordinary...which opened up areas of their own experience to new possibilities'. 'Simply' of course modestly conceals the art of the teacher who must call into being that openness which allows the 'new possibilities' to come to fruition. Emma Walkey's poem captures the spirit of the orchard out of the sensuous detail that is a matter of her own recorded observation. It is a fantasy but it is distilled from ordinary perceptions that have passed through the imagination to be revealed as a mystery:

> Her breath is the mist on cold morning air,
> As her dry silk ball gown, moth eaten, brushes past
> Dead trees and wilting flowers.
> She smells of cider and mothballs
> And apples in wicker baskets,
> Tunnelled by wasps.

This, I think, illustrates what Ted Hughes meant when, in attempting to describe 'the characteristic Halesworth imprint', he speaks of

> a certain overtone which the style carries. This overtone expresses the effort – the constantly renewed and intensely focused effort – to be precise and honest in observation and word, and to infuse all perceptions with a personal, first-hand guarantee.
>
> (Pirrie, 1987, p.x)

Emma has clearly come to feel the English language to be her own, to be a gift she can explore in giving shape to her inner life. And giving shape to her inner life involves close reference to the material facts of nature upon which it depends for sustenance. Can we imagine that a child who uses her native language in this concentrated and careful way will have any trouble with other kinds of writing: with 'analysis, hypothesis, recollection, explanation' and all those other categories the 1995 Order misleadingly separates from writing 'for aesthetic and imaginative purposes'? She has already found her standard and her aim in the 'inheritance' that is shaping her own expression. As has Stephen Gardam in 'Fox'. In his case the immediate provenance of the poem is Ted Hughes' 'The Thought-Fox'. Stephen's work is indebted to Hughes but rises from it in the strong imagining of his own creature:

> Cautiously he edges out on to the log:
> Tail raised for balance.
> One of his first few steps slips
> On the thin wet moss.
> It starts to rain heavily;
> His fur is drenched, and is stood on end,
> Clustered in spikes.

The character of the teaching is palpable here: the insistence on scrupulousness of observation and crisp, apt word and phrase. This cannot be reduced to a 'method' but Blishen supplies the clue when, having watched Jill Pirrie at work, he speaks of the characteristic activity of 'giving attention, for a packed ten minutes or so, to a poem or story that demonstrably has no laziness or staleness in it'. It is a matter, in that phrase Bellow quotes from Tolstoy, of 'breeding attentiveness' in pupil writers and, thus, in their readers.

The 'habit of looking hard', the 'exorcising of cliché', the 'intolerance of idleness of language' (Blishen's phrases) are the background to writing of this quality. What typically we find in these poems is that the 'looking hard' has registered in close, economic and sharply expressed observation; observation has released the sympathies that come with the imaginative effort to see and represent the object as it really is. The poems achieve 'breadth through focus' (Pirrie, 1993b). These children are aware, for instance, of the brevity and frequent brutality of the lives of the animals on which we depend. They are 'entirely unsentimental'. But that is not enough, for 'it is all too easy to take so much for granted and country children must learn to look in ways that regenerate thought and feeling'. The conclusion of Kirsty Butcher's 'The Cow':

> The cow, a beautiful caring creature;
> And we take her milk,
> And sometimes her calf and her life.

is powerful and troubling not because she has argued her way to it but because she has evoked that beauty and that life in all that precedes those final lines:

> Ears folded like wrinkled-up shavings;
> Softly smiling mouth with strings of spit
> Hanging from the gentle pinkness of lips.

Contemplating writing of this quality, one sees more readily the truth of Jill Pirrie's remark that 'often the teacher's role must be that of a narrower down, rather than an opener up. Paradoxically, when the possibilities are narrowed down, they open up in remarkable ways. Always imagination must be anchored in reality' (Pirrie, 1987). To have looked hard in the way demonstrated in these poems, to have had one's sympathies awakened or expanded, is to have grown in moral understanding. This is 'the regeneration of thought and feeling': that is, not the implanting of 'correct' attitudes but the development of sensibility. 'Only when children achieve the relaxed intensity in which they are thrown on their own resources in an act of memory which returns them to their own narrow world are they freed to write well' (Pirrie, 1993a):

> Dark red pipes and tubes
> Moving as the chick lies,
> Mouth wide, gasping for breath,
> Eyes half-closed,
> Legs kicking widely into space.
> Clawing for a hold.

The poem concludes:

> I murmur a prayer
> As other chicks use it
> To clamber over,
> The sticky grey tinsel
> No longer fluffy.

> I go for a shovel.

('Chicken Lucky' by Caroline English)

Jill Pirrie says of the endings of poems such as this that 'there is often a moment of appropriation, as though all those issues of time, death, finality, are at last, for the moment at least, brought under control in an eminently matter-of-fact way' (Pirrie, 1993b). Absent from such poems is not just sentimentality but attitudinizing of any kind. You never feel you are reading the expression of 'views'; what these children are doing is developing sensibility in ways which, when they come to articulate them in discursive terms, will give their views an authenticity, a rootedness, that saves them from abstraction. Those who think that 'mastery' comes from increasingly differentiated descriptions and teaching of 'skills' are answered in *Apple Fire*. For what distinguishes Jill Pirrie's English is that it is cultural through and through. Language is not a skill; it is one of the forms of being. *Apple Fire* is rich proof of the kinship of literacy and literature. In Jill Pirrie's philosophy of English teaching, language, culture and experience are interrelated in ways that severely call in question the dismemberments to which they are subjected in National Curriculum English. For Jill Pirrie, 'it is in the company of the poet and the storyteller that children come into their rightful inheritance'. This, for her, is 'the rigorous route to literacy'. These children are 'learning to think, look and listen within' that company; they are 'developing the ability to discriminate, adapt and criticize' as 'a natural by-product of developing thought, feeling and sensibility'. Grammar is not dispensed with; indeed how could it be? It is an indispensable part of their inheritance but it is not something held apart from the 'forms and symbols of the language'.

In speaking of the poems in *On Common Ground*, Ted Hughes said that English teaching of this kind must, in the end, 'have its pervasive effect on the whole mentality and well-being'. It is the central tenet of Jill Pirrie's teaching and of the tradition she represents:

> Moreover Literature inculcates such consciousness of language that the power to reflect transfers readily and easily to [these] other genres practised within other disciplines. It is the English teacher's responsibility to equip children with the necessary criteria for reflection, rather than provide opportunities for practice. These opportunities already exist across the curriculum. Within the English classroom, an account of a process will be literary. Ultimately, this is to make that classroom truly inclusive as children learn to discriminate and transform as surely as they inform. Only the literary genre is so truly catholic in application and therefore so empowering. It is never just another means by which human-beings communicate. To believe this is a huge abdication of responsibility on the part of the English teacher.
>
> (Pirrie, 1994, pp.105–106)

There, indisputably, speaks professional judgement. 'There needs' (said the NCC in its 1993 Consultation Report on proposals for the revision of the 1990 Order) to be 'a proper balance between professional judgement and statutory requirement'. It sounds judicious and proper. 'Balance' is a word that comes with its own seal of approval. But what if the factors in question should not *be* balanced? What if 'statutory requirement' is fundamentally at odds with 'professional judgement'? What kind of balance is desirable between 'professional judgement' and ideas that are wrong? Applied to either the 1990 or the Revised Order, Jill Pirrie's judgement (as it speaks in the passage quoted) makes the question unavoidable. What balance is possible between that philosophy of English teaching and the Council's 1993 view that a level 8 student (exhibiting a 'sophisticated choice of syntax and vocabulary') might

> Write two contrasting pieces (eg. on a personal experience). One in the first person should use simple, direct sentences with active verbs and a deliberately uncomplicated structure and grammar; the second should comment on the experience ironically or humorously, and the sentences should be expanded with a range of clauses. The tone and viewpoint should be consistent.
>
> (DFE, 1993, p.67)

This is mechanistic pedantry, an impediment to the 'distinctive personal style' students are required to develop. If an experience is 'personal' we expect a strong sense of personality in the writing. Where is the personality whose irony and humour will survive, let alone feel free to express themselves, in the prosaic prison house of that 'extended range of clauses'? This is a particularly blatant example of the nonsense that arises from placing mechanics before meaning. It is utterly *un*sophisticated in that it is untouched by knowledge and experience of English prose. Writers certainly tend to work within the syntactical rhythms prevailing in their own cultures; but no writer ever thought a 'distinctive personal style' lay within a pattern so precisely determined.

'Only when we eschew the comfortable concessions of the National Curriculum which separates language and literature can we restore value and vision' (Pirrie, 1994). There is much in the 1995 Order that works against such a restoration. The document is slimmer than its predecessor but the philosophy is much the same. The 'dissociation of sensibility' remains: the 'Writing' section of the Order is closed off from and unaffected by the standards implicit in the 'major works of literature' that must be studied. There is neither 'value' nor 'vision' in the requirement that pupils' writing at the highest levels should 'show the selection of specific features or expressions to convey particular effects' and 'show control of a range of styles maintaining the interest of the reader throughout'.

What, it might be asked, is 'comfortable' about schemes of assessment which require teachers to examine children's writing for evidence of 'adaptation of style and register to different forms' (level 6) or of their ability to develop a style in which, successively, 'words are chosen for variety and interest' (level 3), 'words are used for effect' (level 4) and 'words are used precisely' (level 5)? There, surely, is what Ted Hughes calls 'the spiritless pedantry of the inane', graphically exemplified in SEAC's previously awarding credit to 'the ability to recognize variation in vocabulary according to purpose, topic and audience'. The piece in question (the Ancient Mariner's log-book) was dull but the boy's vocabulary was 'varied': 'he uses words like "enthusiasm", "exotic", "landscape" and "re-appears" appropriately' (a criterion easily satisfied by the trashiest writing). I have myself witnessed a child being advised to hoist himself up a 'level' in the new Order by working a 'more impressive' vocabulary into an already accomplished piece! The absence of 'value and vision' discourages initiative, imagination and independent thought and makes for an English that is 'manageable' only at the cost of being dull and uninspired. What is the use of children being taught 'the differences between speech and writing' or being 'taught about variation in the written forms and how these differ from spoken forms' (DFE, 1995)? The tone is portentous; the result can too easily be mediocrity. Can we really justify (in the name of 'looking at the differences between speech and writing') reading extracts from *The Beano*, studying children's transcribed opinions about it and then asking pupils how they 'would know without being told' that the transcription 'was speech written down and not something someone had written'? (Seely and Kitchen, 1995). The earnest taxonomies and abstractions (in the 'Writing' section as elsewhere) stifle rather than awaken our sense of what good English teaching is like, of the importance indeed of the teacher: of conviction, of passion, of example. Jill Pirrie's example shows us where, come the next revision of National Curriculum English, we might look for renewal.

CHAPTER SIX
Standard English and the Spoken Word

In the churchyard of St Denys, Evington, on the outskirts of Leicester, there is a memorial headstone to William Hallowell and his family. The headstone was erected by Mr and Mrs Keck of Stoughton Grange:

TO PERPETUATE THE REGARD
IN WHICH THEY HOLD THE MEMORY
OF FAITHFUL DOMESTICS AND DEPENDANTS.
WILLIAM HALLOWELL WAS BUTLER
TO G.A. KECK, ESQ.
WITH WHOM HE LIVED TWELVE YEARS
ESTEEMED FOR ABILITY, INTEGRITY, ATTACHMENT AND ZEAL
HE DIED
JANUARY 23 AD 1816, AGED 39 YEARS
AFFECTIONATELY REGRETTED.

The words 'Ability, Integrity, Attachment and Zeal' have the weight and dignity that belongs to the much longer inscription of which they are a part. That weight and dignity are in the words because they are *behind* the words; the confidence with which they are used belongs to a culture in which moral abstractions of this kind have come to possess an almost concrete force. What lies behind those words is the Augustan tradition in prose and verse, whose representative figure is Dr Samuel Johnson. Johnson was a one man academy, attempting, in his dictionary (1755), to establish norms that would enable an entire people to know more precisely what it was talking about. He is a force behind that tombstone inscription as he is behind the writing of Jane Austen. William Hallowell died two years after the publication of *Mansfield Park* (1814). The 'attachment' for which he is praised and commemorated combines the ideas of loyalty and affection, as in Jane Austen's description of a woman as 'So totally unamiable, so absolutely incapable of attaching a sensible man' (*Sense and Sensibility*, 1811). It is by this time a word of such clarity and moral weight, of deliberately limited and concentrated meaning, as to allow for the delicious irony Jane Austen works into her description of one of the Ward sisters in *Mansfield Park* who 'found herself obliged to be attached to the Reverend Mr Norris'.

Of course if you are *obliged* to be attached, you are not attached at all in the meaning of the word as we see it both on the Hallowell headstone and in *Sense and Sensibility*. What makes for the irony of Mrs Norris's fate is that the positive human meaning plays against the functional meanings of 'attached' – meanings that have undoubtedly become much stronger since Jane Austen's day (the influence of technology means that it is *things* rather than persons that we primarily think of in relation to the word). We can accurately speak of a language here having achieved a maturity that makes possible both the dignity of the tombstone inscription and the irony of Jane Austen. The joint examples reflect a level of cultural unity: the language of William Hallowell's memorial, one imagines, would have been understood and appreciated across the land. Not all of those who understood it would have been able to read Jane Austen but people at every level of society would have benefited from a language developed to the point where those great moral abstractions – 'Ability, Integrity, Attachment and Zeal' – felt like facts of nature.

Here we see the civilizing strength of a 'standard' language and, incidentally, the grounds for making the literature of the past an essential component of English in the National Curriculum. We can still read and be moved by the words on that headstone as we can be moved and delighted by Jane Austen. To reflect on either is to appreciate the elements both of continuity and provisionality in the English language: 'ability, integrity, attachment and zeal' are all usable words but their usage and meanings have of course changed ('zeal' is now all but *un*usable, it seems, except facetiously). To discuss such changes in the context of reading good fiction is part of the essential work of English teaching, of developing that 'moral and emotional understanding' referred to in the new Order (DFE, 1995). This phrase, however, is not an altogether happy one. 'Emotional' suggests an activity of the mind somehow separate from 'thought', whereas in Jane Austen it is the strength of thought *and* feeling, the one indissociable from the other, of which we are conscious. (Significantly and very unhelpfully, the Order lists 'the development of thinking' as but one of the 'purposes' for which 'pupils should be given opportunities to talk' (DFE, 1995).)

If we say that the Augustan tradition underlies the strength and moral confidence of Jane Austen's prose, we are acknowledging its debt to a sustained and broadly-based effort towards the precise articulation of meaning. It is not the only way: no one will now accuse Shakespeare (emphatically not an Augustan) of imprecision, but within the Augustan tradition (one thinks of Dryden, Pope, Gray, Cowper) there is characteristically an intense clarity of expression born, it seems, of the very constraints that it imposes. Inevitably now we are much more keenly conscious than Dr Johnson's contemporaries of what such constraints exclude. Johnson indeed was far from being a totally benign influence on the English language. The severity of his judgements on popular idiom (he dismissed the 'dictions' of 'the laborious and mercantile part of the people' as 'fugitive cant' which could not 'be regarded as any of the durable materials of a language' (Smith, 1984)), the often oppressively latinate weight of his own prose and the very definitiveness implied in the production of his dictionary would all inevitably come to be challenged. Imitation of the style of writing they encouraged was too easy. The very concentration of meaning made possible in the development of a standard English such as we find it in the eighteenth century excludes other ranges of meaning – those to be heard, for instance, in regional speech. Equally, the standard forms (by which of course is implied syntactical regularities as well as vocabulary) may become instruments of obfuscation and evasion rather than of concentration and clarification. They may as readily constrain as enrich expression, as readily stifle as release the individual voice. The prose style of Kazuo Ishiguro's *The Remains of the Day* (1989) exploits this tendency to fascinating effect, from the very first words of the book: 'It seems increasingly likely that I really will undertake the expedition that has been preoccupying my imagination now for some days'. If Johnson was a force behind those words commemorating the real life butler, William Hallowell, he is still an influence on Ishiguro's fictional butler, Stevens. The butler writes and speaks an English that accurately reflects his impeccable standards of personal and professional conduct. But it is an English that belongs to another time. His time is the 1950s and he is recalling the 1930s but his English belongs in the nineteenth century. As actually, psychologically, does he. He is marooned in a view of the world which no longer matches the larger, political world that impinges on his life. He has, so to speak, taken refuge in a standardized version of English which is also a standardized view of the world: in his case it incapacitates him emotionally as well as morally, making it as impossible for him to talk with women as it is for him to grasp what is happening in the world around him. If butlers have their 'fugitive cant', Stevens is extraordinarily successful in excising it from his own story.

Standard forms of a language are in one way the indisputable signs of high civilization. There is, however, an inherent weakness in them: they are permanently in danger of producing standardized expression which falls well short of the standards achieved by the greatest and most individualistic exponents of those forms. The important thing is to know when this is happening. George Orwell's strictures on standard English are still very much to the point. Once we have developed a degree of facility with its forms we find it all too easy to manipulate them mechanically, as does the butler in Ishiguro's novel. Orwell, of course, was constantly drawing attention to the ways in which such manipulations served the purposes of propaganda and rhetoric. He was concerned too that a facility with the written forms tends to carry over into speech; that the standardizing tendency infects those less reflective, more spontaneous impulses to expression that issue in the spoken word – impulses that need to be nurtured rather than constrained:

> But probably the deadliest enemy of good English is what is called standard English. This dreary dialect, the language of leading articles, white papers, political speeches and BBC news bulletins is undoubtedly spreading; it is spreading downwards in the social scale and outwards into the spoken language. Its characteristic is its reliance on ready-made phrases...spoken English when it tries to be dignified and logical usually takes on the vices of written English, as you can see by spending half an hour either in the House of Commons or at Marble Arch.
>
> (Orwell and Angus, 1982, pp.43–44)

Things have certainly not improved in the half-century that separates us from this observation. Students reading *Animal Farm* with a teacher who knows and draws upon Orwell's seminal essay 'Politics and the English Language' (1960) will be learning to detect the symptoms of the decline he describes. They may also appreciate the irony that, in a National Curriculum calling for 'an integrated programme of Speaking and Listening, Reading and Writing', a reliance on 'ready-made phrases' may be quite enough to win you high credit in the first of those elements. Ishiguro's butler 'shows confident use of standard English in situations that require it' and it is difficult to imagine Orwell's politicians and public speakers being unequal to the demands made upon those aiming to be credited with 'exceptional performance': they 'show assured and fluent use of standard English in a range of situations and for a variety of purposes' (DFE, 1995). These 'level descriptions' are seriously deficient in that they totally eschew the question of quality. They can as easily accommodate bad as good English. This is inevitable once the error is made of equating standard with good English. The 1992 'Case' for the revision of the 1990 Order asked that 'references to the mastery of standard English' should be 'strengthened'. To encourage children to 'use standard English in conversation' would be to 'encourage them to speak clearly, accurately and confidently' (NCC, 1992). A year later, in a disingenuous play on words, the notions of standard English and rising standards were conflated: 'An emphasis on speaking standard English is essential if standards of spoken English are to be raised' (NCC, 1993). The celebratory words of Patsy Rodenburg (Head of the Voice Department at the National Theatre) about the present-day variety of spoken English and the syntax-threatening unorthodoxy of lively, truly engaged conversation are an excellent corrective to the suggestion that such vitality must express itself through the standard forms. Moreover hers is an 'integrated understanding': she sees, as the authors of the new English Order do not, how literature itself can teach us about the spoken word:

> What makes the speaking of English so wonderful nowadays is its sheer dynamism and variety. In fact the great oral tradition is probably kept most alive on the street. If you spend a day wandering round London you will hear the rhythm of it shifting in all directions as so-called 'standard' variants merge with East End Cockney, Irish, Australian, American, Bengali, Rasta talk, African variants and dozens of other distinct native sounds. When we are speaking most naturally and most comfortably, we return to our native accent for ease and familiarity. And in that accent we are often most eloquent...
>
> Need instantly creates its own set of rules and conditions. The cry from the heart may not neatly match the laws of syntax and word order. Shakespeare and every other great writer of poetry and plays writes just as much, and in some cases more, for the speaking voice rather than for a reader's eye.
>
> (Rodenburg, 1993, pp.47–48)

One remembers that George Eliot's Adam Bede 'whenever he wished to be especially kind to his mother, fell into his strongest native accent and dialect' (Eliot, 1922). Indeed, to contemplate the heritage of literature written in English is vividly to appreciate that a good measure of its richness derives from the immense expressive variety of the spoken language and the correspondingly rich range of perception and observation thus made available to readers of English. Many teachers of English have in recent years drawn enthusiastically and profitably on this expressive diversity (appropriately enough in a country now marked by unprecedented ethnic diversity too). 'Professional judgement' has itself been educated through experiment with and experience of that diversity. For many English teachers 'the study of texts which explore the complexities of personal experience [and] should play a major part in the development of the moral understanding and appreciation of our cultural heritage' (NCC, 1992) will nowadays quite properly embrace, for example, writers such as Alice Walker, Toni Morrison, Edward Brathwaite, Derek Walcott, Maya Angelou, Chinua Achebe. These writers have enriched the language, changed our sense of its achievement and potentialities and sharpened our sense of its expressive reach.

To contemplate the 'cultural heritage' in this light, and thus to heighten one's sense of the complicated relationship between the spoken and the written word within it, is inevitably to find the official equation of 'good English' and 'standard spoken English' quaint, purblind and frustrating. Standard English is of course indispensable to a modern, industrialized and bureaucratic society. It is indeed central to the achievement of literacy: we communicate and understand one another the better for its unchallenged ascendancy in written English. In education it is thus the dominant form, whether in writing or in teachers' speech. These are truisms, of obvious general relevance to teachers of all subjects but leaving us to work out our answer to the important question: what, in the matter of the spoken word, is the distinctive contribution we should expect from 'English'? The new Order for English offers no help:

> Pupils should be taught to be fluent, accurate users of standard English vocabulary and grammar, and to recognize its importance as the language of public communication. They should be taught to adapt their talk to suit the circumstances, and to be confident users of standard English in formal and informal situations.

> (DFE, 1995, p.18)

To ask where we find the imprint of the 'cultural heritage' on such statements; to ask in what degree they are responsive to the 'sheer dynamism and variety' of current spoken English, is to show them up in all their soulless instrumentality. How have we come to this?

In his 1987 pamphlet, *English our English* (published by the government's Centre for Policy Studies), John Marenbon attempted a description of 'the new orthodoxy' he claimed to be disfiguring the teaching of English. Amongst the supposed tenets of this orthodoxy Marenbon highlighted the belief that 'no language or dialect is inherently superior to any other'. The consequence, he declared, was that 'by devaluing standard English, the new orthodoxy is destroying it'. Marenbon's pamphlet appeared shortly after the Kingman Committee began its work and some two years before the Cox Report (strongly influenced by Kingman) laid the foundations for the first National Curriculum English Order. Marenbon expressed the hope that the 'politicians and committees' preparing for the introduction of the Order would 'keep strong in their common sense, distrustful of experts and chaste towards fashion'. By the time of the 1992 'Case' the government had evidently concluded that Marenbon's hope had been misplaced: that intellectual fashion had not only triumphed over common sense but over the 'experts' too. The 1993 Proposals for a Revised Order were accordingly marked by unprecedentedly open political intervention. The 'experts' having supposedly embraced the 'new orthodoxy' (in fact there are sensible observations about standard English in both Kingman and Cox), the government would in fundamental ways take the direction of English into its own hands. Each member of the 'Review Team' that produced the proposals had 'taught English extensively'; but, tellingly, its work was overseen by a 'Review Group' (headed by NCC's chairman) 'which guided the detailed work from a policy perspective' (NCC, 1993): an ominous phrase. The implication is clear: the Review Team wrote to order. Standard English would henceforth be the watchword, the straightforwardly intelligible, formative principle that would unify practice and raise standards in the subject. Government exasperation was concentrated upon the failure of an endeavour to define what children should 'know about language': the LINC project. With LINC it seemed clear to the government that, far from providing the expected resistance to such relativism, those responsible for the project had proved themselves complicit in the very evils it had been set up to reform (Eggar, 1991). The government's summary rejection of the materials associated with the project set the tone of its interventions in the years leading to the revision of the National Curriculum Order for English. Standard English became an emblem of resistance to the thoroughgoing linguistic and cultural relativism of which LINC stood accused and which, it was clearly felt, neither the English teaching profession nor those charged with giving it direction had done enough to withstand.

Marenbon's claim that the 'new orthodoxy' was 'destroying' standard English is patently false; he offered no evidence to support the claim. What he did, essentially, was strike an attitude. That attitude (again not, on the evidence, supported by analytical understanding) was echoed in the School Curriculum and Assessment Authority's deputy chief executive's claim that the proposals for 'Standard English and the English literary heritage are designed to reinforce a common culture' (Tate, 1994). Whilst there are indeed still many teachers who would see the sharing and transmission of the 'literary heritage' as a principal means of establishing 'a common culture', few would accept that this heritage is synonymous with standard English. Both historical and contemporary examples offer vivid correctives to this equation. Historically the emblematic case is that of John Clare (a prescribed author in the new Order and thus beyond dispute as part of the heritage). Clare's first publishers trimmed and polished the native Northamptonshire speech of his poems; reviewers scorned his 'provincialisms' as a sign of his 'wretched taste and poverty of thought' (Paulin, 1990). In our own time the tensions between the standard forms of the language and such 'provincialisms' have themselves become the creative source, indeed the very stuff of some of the most provoking and memorable writing in English. Such writing is part of the consciousness of many teachers of English, part indeed of *their* heritage. That consciousness cannot be expected to disavow itself. It includes a much subtler, historically more informed sensitivity to the nature and function of the standard forms of the English language than it finds reflected in the official prescriptions. It is highly likely, for instance, to include a knowledge of the poetry of Tony Harrison.

Tony Harrison is a key figure in this debate. Harrison's is an unsettling poetry, consistently and often shockingly checking the habits of mind that dispose us to favour standard English as intrinsically good English; consistently reminding us that, as a matter of common humanity, we need to think more sensitively, more historically if we are properly to value the English language and those who use it. Harrison supplies the historical and cultural dimension lacking in official pronouncement and prescription for National Curriculum English. There are probably few readers who will be able to get through his poem 'Working' without the assistance of the Oxford English Dictionary. The speaker in 'this sonnet for the bourgeoisie' stares into the fire and imagines a figure in the history of the coal on which it depends: Patience Kershaw, 'bald hurryer, fourteen', already physically ruined by harsh, sunless, unrelenting work amongst the 'stooped getters' of the coal. The poem is an act of remembrance, not only for a forgotten individual but for a forgotten or derided tongue, a native idiom. In a startling and fine concluding couplet Harrison collapses the various levels of the poem's meaning into a single statement:

> wherever hardship held its tongue the job
> 's breaking the silence of the worked-out-gob.

Harrison himself supplies the gloss on the word 'gob': 'an old Northern coal-mining word for the space left after the coal has been extracted. Also, of course, the mouth, and speech'. The tongue that was held is now released through the words of the poet. The tension and the effort of physical work are felt in that last line with an immediacy that belongs to the language of the poem as a whole. Harrison works with the strong, unadorned, physically immediate vernacular. Patience (the name so apposite for one who held her tongue) Kershaw's work is described in a vocabulary it now needs a dictionary to explain. It is a vocabulary that has gone the way of the life it recalls and the way of those who lived it and were exhausted through it: the 'worked-out-gob' has to be *imagined* back into life. Harrison may (as he says in another poem, 'Wordlists II') feel estranged from 'the tongue that once I used to know/but can't bone up on now'. But 'Working' *is* a 'boning up', a recovery of language. Patience Kershaw's 'skinned skull shines' as the speaker, closing his eyes ('that makes a dark like mines'), imagines her:

> Among stooped getters, grimy, knacker-bare,
> head down thrusting a 3 cwt corf
> turned your crown bald, your golden hair
> chafed fluffy first and then scuffed off,
> chick's back, then eggshell, that sunless white.
> You strike sparks and plenty but can't see.

(Harrison, 1987, p.124)

The sparks struck by Patience are struck again in the poet's violently illuminating words. The energy of the language in 'Working' is the energy of the vernacular, of words used in intimate association with the physical acts and circumstances that have called them into being. Words like 'getters', 'grimy', 'knacker', 'corf', 'scuffed', 'strike', 'sparks', 'skinned', 'skull', 'gob' belong to the hardy, earthbound, practical part of our linguistic inheritance. They are amongst what Logan Pearsall Smith called 'those vigorous expressions which have come to us from popular speech and which still seem to carry, like overtones, some sense of the acts and occasions which gave them birth' (Pearsall Smith, 1943).

That we now need to consult our dictionaries in order to understand some of these expressions, that 'Working' relies upon a readership schooled in the word-play on which its meaning depends, is a keen and clearly intended irony. 'Breaking the silence' is a 'job' that calls for the collaboration of the poet and his reader. Only through a combined effort to re-animate the vernacular, to re-establish something of an oral culture within which Patience Kershaw and her fellow 'getters' had their being, can they be restored to our understanding. Moreover, within the revived vernacular there is an implicit challenge to the abstract standard English sonorities of the historian or economist. Simultaneously, we ('educated' readers that we are) are left with a sense that we are habitually too hospitable to those sonorities (in which the Patience Kershaws tend to figure only as shadowy symbols of their class) and that, in living too comfortably within the habits of mind they derive from and promote, we have become dull to the experience that alone gives them what meaning they possess. These are the habits of mind George Orwell was referring to when he described standard English as 'probably the deadliest enemy of good English':

> 'Educated' English has grown anaemic because for long past it has not been re-invigorated from below. The people likeliest to use simple concrete language, and to think of metaphors that really call up a visual image, are

those who are in contact with physical reality...And the vitality of English depends on a steady supply of images of this kind.

(Orwell and Angus, 1982, pp.43–44)

Harrison's poem enacts Orwell's perception. The oral culture within which Patience Kershaw had her being knew nothing of the sophistication ('You are lost in this sonnet for the bourgeoisie') with which her suffering is evoked. However, without that illiterate culture the tribute could not be made. Harrison's achievement is to make us feel that the springs of sympathy lie in the English that was native to that culture and that standard English is the poorer without it. Furthermore, and late in the day, we must remain deliberately, stubbornly in touch with such an English if we too are to connect with our own personal and cultural histories. The deliberateness is necessary because the overwhelming tendency is for the language to become more abstract, generalized, standardized.

As an 'educated speaker' *and* a poet, Harrison is attuned to the histories of the various linguistic codes that constitute his own English. No such historical sensitivity complicates the National Curriculum view of standard English. We cannot read Tony Harrison (part now, surely, of the 'cultural heritage') with young people, cannot help them to become attuned to those histories, and agree that 'an emphasis on communicating fluently and confidently in spoken standard English is essential if standards of spoken English are to be raised' (NCC, 1992). The morally neutral qualities of fluency and confidence apart (one may be confident, fluent and *vacuous* in standard as in any other form of English!), how shall we recognise good spoken English when we hear it? Where do we get *our* standards from in judging that? Teachers will look in vain for answers to these questions in the revised Order for National Curriculum English.

Without historical perspective and sensitivity we cannot think clearly about the spoken word and standard English. Tony Harrison's poetry is poetry to think with. His subtle and deeply felt explorations of the relations between our native language and our sense of identity are a true guide. It is guidance arising out of perception, experience, reflection and judgement. The National Curriculum guidance is of a different order: 'The richness of dialects and other languages can make an important contribution to pupils' knowledge and understanding of standard English' (DFE, 1995). This doesn't help us to think clearly at all. Nonetheless it gets straight into the coursebooks: 'to develop your understanding of dialect and standard English...think about the dialect that people in your area speak. Make a list of words and expressions that people use. Against each one write what it means in standard English'. Similarly, 'go through the poem, trying to work out what each dialect word would be in standard

English' (Seely and Kitchen, 1995). Unless such exercises are controlled by a deeper understanding of the purposes they serve (an understanding absent from the National Curriculum document) they are little more than shallow diversions. If, in the classroom, we read Lawrence's deservedly much anthologized 'A Collier's Wife':

> Somebody's knocking at the door
>   Mother, come down and see,
> – I's think it's nobbut a beggar,
>   Say, I'm busy

we don't do so in order to increase 'pupils' knowledge and understanding of standard English'. We read it for its expressive, human qualities – qualities indissociable from the dialect in which it is written. The teacher's task is to assist the work of the poem, to ensure that it is truly heard and understood for what it is: the native accents of the speakers in Lawrence's poem are the accents through which he expresses his own sympathies and awakens ours. What we 'know and understand' about standard English here (implicitly of course) is its limitations: its weakness (in contrast to 'the richness of dialect') in registering the pulse of human feeling and response. Children are undoubtedly able to feel the force of that contrast; they do not need to consider 'the vocabulary and grammar of standard English and dialectal variations' in separate programmes of study (in 'Speaking and Listening') on the development of English (DFE, 1995).

We can confidently include Lawrence and Tony Harrison in that long line of good judges (writers and critics) who do not see 'a common culture' based on the spread of standard English as an unmixed blessing. That education should reinforce such a culture would not have been the view of the collector of dialect words who in 1865 complained that 'an excellent clergyman and an energetic schoolmaster are committing irreparable mischief by teaching the people to read' (Pearsall Smith, 1943). What this superficially facetious complaint registered was an irresistible tendency towards standardization that was to become the frequent subject of regret amongst those who understood that the health of a national language is in no small degree dependent upon that of its local varieties. 'Since that time' (i.e. 1865), wrote Pearsall Smith, 'excellent clergymen and energetic schoolmasters have certainly waged a war on local words not unlike that war waged by gamekeepers on many species of wild birds'. Pearsall Smith was in no doubt about the power of the standard language to block up the sources of its own vitality. Regretting 'that superstitious feeling of awe and respect for standard English which is now being spread by the diffusion of education', he was aware that the native liveliness of speech tends to suffer, to lose its idiomatic force, once it comes under the influence of the written language:

> A standard language moreover, is, under modern conditions, a written rather than a spoken language. The printed word becomes more and more the reality, the spoken word an echo or faint copy of it. This inversion of the normal relation between speech and writing, this predominance of the eye over the ear, of the written symbol over its audible equivalent, tends to deprive the language of that vigour and reality which comes, and can only come, from its intimate association with the acts and passions of men, as they vividly describe and express them in their speech.
>
> (Pearsall Smith, 1943, p.163)

Numerous writers have been troubled by the impact of a national educational system on local speech. The homogenizing effect of standard English has often been seen as threatening to impoverish rather than to 'raise standards in' the spoken language. Introducing the Dorset dialect poems of William Barnes, Thomas Hardy remarked that, since Barnes' death in 1886,

> education in the west of England as elsewhere has gone on with its silent and inevitable effacements, reducing the speech of this country to uniformity, and obliterating every year many a fine old local word. The process is always the same: the word is ridiculed by the newly taught; it gets into disgrace; it is heard in holes and corners only; it dies; and worst of all, it leaves no synonym.
>
> (Motion, 1994, p.145)

Edwin Muir's reflection on the 'effacements' suffered by 'the idiom of the Orkney language' are in the same vein. It has 'been ironed out by the Educational System'. 'The islands produce a terrible number of professors. But simple, uneducated people here and there still speak a beautiful language and know where to set a word in a sentence' (Muir, 1954).

What unites those various commentators is the recognition that good spoken English is not the sole possession of the educated speaker; that, indeed, his education may unfit him unless the standard English he encounters and uses is nourished and sustained by idiomatic sources of the quality variously registered by Hardy, Muir, Orwell and Harrison. The books of George Ewart Evans record the 'vitality of English' as it is to be found in 'the sayings of country people, always rich in concrete images and braced with the vigour and rhythm that gives them long life'. Like Orwell, Evans saw that the health of the standard language depended upon regular infusions of such vigour: dialect was 'a clear reservoir of spoken language which can enrich and purify the modern tongue' (Evans, 1971). Education has tended (those commentators are agreed) to be hostile to such sources, to be suspicious of what Jespersen called 'that tyrannical, capricious, utterly incalculable thing, idiomatic usage' (Jespersen, 1922). English is full of 'idiomatic transgressions' of 'the rules of grammar' and the 'rules of logic', transgressions made acceptable by usage but still the target of denunciation in 'books on good English' where – according to Pearsall Smith (1943) – we will find 'these wild creatures of talk, nailed up, like noxious birds and vermin, by the purists and preservers of our speech'. It is interesting to see Pearsall Smith (like Patsy Rodenburg half a century on – and long before his metaphors would have been examined for what they tell us about language and power) registering the subversive energies of the idioms he records. The anomalies of grammar and syntax to be found in those idioms are representative of the energies which gave birth to them: energies impatient to find a form which will vividly express the dominant feeling by which they are coloured, a form which obviously will not be determined by the regularities of grammar, syntax and vocabulary in which we recognize the standard language. Such an understanding is altogether absent from the National Curriculum. By 1993 good spoken English had become, in the official mind, written standard English voiced. At the acme of 'competence' in 'Speaking and Listening' (level 10) a pupil would

> speak with flair, creativity and spontaneity in complex situations, with sustained precision and fluency and in consistently accurate standard English.

> (DFE, 1993, p.23)

This is of course radically contradictory: to dictate terms to 'flair, creativity and spontaneity' (words embracing the unplanned and the unpredictable, that which breaks bounds, exhilarates and disturbs) is to rob them of their meaning. The waywardness noted by Jespersen is the waywardness of life itself, which won't simply come to heel because a government says it should.

For a corrective to so contradictory and constraining an idea of good spoken English we need look no further than 'the major works of literature' prescribed for study in the 1995 Order. 'From Chaucer and Shakespeare to the present', says Margaret Atwood, English Literature 'has been in love with the vernacular, and its best writers have never strayed far from the rhythms and vocabularies of speech' (Ousby, 1992). The indebtedness of the 'literary heritage' to popular speech is abundantly documented in Pearsall Smith's classic study *Words and Idioms* (1943). 'A writer', he says, 'cannot create his own language, he must take what society provides him, and in his search for sensuous and pictured speech he naturally has recourse to the rich and living material created by generations of popular and unconscious artists'. Moreover, the 'metaphorical and grammatical idioms' that can be shown to have made their way from 'humble occupations' into the standard language and into literature are usually 'terse, colloquial, vivid and charged with eager life'; indeed 'just the kind that are sought for and welcomed in animated speech'. In these continuities between a spoken idiom and the native literature we find a principle that might have given coherence to the first National Curriculum Order for English and the revised Order alike. Could there be a more persuasive argument for reading Shakespeare, Keats, Hopkins, D.H. Lawrence or, indeed, any of the classic writers children must study under the revised Order than that their English is 'charged with the eager life' of the idiomatic heritage from which they draw? In studying English of that quality do we not cultivate a feeling for 'good English', written or spoken, as something that cannot be simply equated with the standard forms, however they are defined? It is only in connection with such study that we can speak intelligibly of 'standards of spoken English' being 'raised'.

That such an integrated view of English is absent both from the Revised Order and the 1990 Order suggests that in the matter of speaking and listening we need to reconsider just what it is that we should regard as the distinctive contribution of English. A criticism of the current insistence on spoken standard English (a technical solution to a misconceived 'problem' of declining standards) ought to be able to call upon a richer tradition of understanding and practice in the spoken word than is reflected in either the 1990 or 1995 Orders. To appreciate why this should be seems to me the first step towards restoring an 'integrated understanding' of the subject.

'Keats', said HMI in its excellent *Teaching Poetry in the Secondary School*, knew the value of 'exploratory talk', 'with a sense more of its mystery than its group dynamics'. 'Minds', said Keats, 'leave each other in contrary direction, traverse each other at numberless points and at last greet each other at the journey's end' (HMI, 1986). The best oral work to be found in the schools is sensitive to such insight. There is now, thankfully, a widespread readiness amongst English teachers to value the expressiveness of individuals' speech above its conformity with models of correctness and social acceptability. We have seen a real gain in humanity. Many classrooms are livelier, more productive and more tolerant places as a result. (This is where the work of James Britton and others I discuss in chapter 3 has been most beneficial.) The popularity of

Barry Hines' *Kes* as a text for study in school over the last twenty years or so is wholly apposite in this connection. Under the excitement of talking to a class about his kestrel Billy Casper rose to unpredictable and astonishing levels of eloquence. He rose as well to become a romantic symbol of those imaginative and verbal capacities unregarded in the narrower tradition of English teaching as the inculcation of 'polite' speech. The *teaching* of English has greatly benefited from an increased appreciation of the vastly varied liveliness and power of ordinary speech. Systems of assessment, however, have betrayed it. The very coinage 'oracy', seemingly embodying a new concept, encouraged definitions of the 'skills' by which it was supposedly constituted. The word and the vocabulary it spawned ('oral and aural skills') consolidated a conception of the spoken word and its development in which questions of quality, of discernment, of judgement – those questions essential to 'English' – were of very little account. Dominating both the 1990 and the revised National Curriculum Orders and present in the Bullock Report (DES, 1975) is the assumption that stages of progression in 'Speaking and Listening' are open to precise description and that children's 'performance' may be planned and assessed in the light of them. The splitting off of 'oracy' from a general literacy threatened to sever the spoken word from its moral and cultural roots.

Introducing William Barnes' Dorset poems to the general reader in 1908, Thomas Hardy said there were problems other than those usually encountered in 'the translation of poetry; which to the full is admittedly impossible':

> gesture and facial expression figure so largely in the speech of husbandmen as to be speech itself; hence in the mind's eye of those who know it in its original setting each word of theirs is accompanied by the qualifying face-play which no construing can express.
>
> (Motion, 1994, p.148)

Could there be a more vivid evocation of the subtlety, elusiveness and beauty of speech as a shared, intensely local inheritance? 'Gesture' and 'facial expression' were what the Bullock Report called 'paralinguistic features'. Only a few years later HMI went beyond the stage of recognizing their existence: such 'features', they recommended, should be *taught*: children of eleven should 'in all speaking make appropriate use of eye-contact, gesture, facial expression, pause, tempo and intonation' (DES, 1984). This could not be further removed from Hardy's insight. The 'face-play' he describes was 'almost speech itself', intensifying and integral to the meaning of words; not the conscious invention of individuals but part of a shared language with a continuous history that, as with any language, makes it intelligible to those who use and hear it.

Hardy could never have said of those Dorset dialect speakers that they 'made appropriate use of' that catalogue of 'paralinguistic features'. Such a phraseology represents speakers as exercising deliberate control over their meaning and its reception through the devices and 'skills' at their disposal. Hardy was writing from observation, about a very small community of speakers; HMI was prescribing for speakers across the nation. In striving for 'objectives' that would be intelligible to teachers and attainable by children of all regions and localities (and of a variety of ethnic origins) HMI produced a travesty of the living word.

HMI's strange phraseology was part of an effort to provide teachers with the 'explicit understanding of the nature of spoken language' which the Bullock Report had deemed necessary if they were to acquire the requisite 'high degree of skill in assessing the spoken language of their pupils' (DES, 1975). Bullock had neglected to discuss the *implicit* understanding that teachers already possess and how this relates to the development of the spoken word. Indeed, in this respect Bullock had nothing to say about the teaching of 'English' as a separate discipline. The stress had been upon 'talk' in 'the learning process' and on 'progression' in 'language behaviour'; as such it was no more relevant to English than to any other curriculum subject. Nevertheless, social and behavioural objectives moved to the centre of English teaching and that implicit understanding was smothered beneath them.

In *English for Meaning,* his strongly felt and closely argued critique of the Bullock Report (published four years after that report, in 1979), David Holbrook said that it was 'self-deceiving to believe we can control rather than foster competence, while it will not do to see competence as a mere function apart from the whole emotional life'. By the mid 1980s the separation of competences from 'the whole emotional life' was, at the level of official prescription, complete. 'Oracy' had established itself as the key concept in a distinctive lexicon that sustained the impression that with 'Oral Communication' teachers had entered a new, uncharted and little understood field. To the director of the National Oracy Project the Oral Communication element of GCSE English

> has not proved controversial...This is probably the consequence of the compromise which left it separately (and differently) graded within the examining system. It has become such an accepted – or disregarded – part of GCSE that it is very difficult to find out what standards students are achieving nationally.
>
> (Norman, Ed., 1992)

The note of uncertainty and the relaxed acceptance of the difficulty are sharply at variance with the tone and promise of the public statements of the mid 1980s. A standardized idiom for the discussion of the spoken word was then emerging, an idiom shaped partly by the need to demonstrate 'what standards students are achieving nationally.' That speech is an elusive, variegated and chameleon creature which will not be pinned down for dispassionate examination is a truth that the standardizing idiom obscured or denied. 'Words', said Tennyson, 'like Nature, half-reveal/And half-conceal the Soul within'. The dominant idiom, shaped by 'assessment considerations', was unaffected by such an insight:

> The grade 1 candidate can be expected to have demonstrated competence: deploying a range of speech styles appropriate to audience and situation and taking responsibility for or contributing considerably to the maintenance of an appropriate atmosphere to facilitate effective communication.
>
> (Northern Examining Association, 1986)

The misbegotten desire for objectivity engenders a vocabulary that, ostensibly precise, is jarringly inappropriate to the teaching of English as an expressive and imaginative discipline. The dulled rhythms and bureaucratic phrases that dominate this typical prescription compose a painful irony: they are unmarked by the cadences of speech, by the very essence of what they profess to describe. What we hear instead is, in Tom Paulin's words, 'the uptight, efficient voice of Official Standard':

> the vernacular imagination distrusts print in the way that most of us dislike legal documents. That imagination expresses itself in speech and feels trammelled by the monolithic simplicities of print, by those formulaic monotonies which distort the spirit of the living language.
>
> (Paulin, 1994, p.xxi).

In their remote, standardizing impersonality the GCSE syllabuses of the mid 1980s already seem to advertise the folly of attempting to legislate for, define and assess the spoken word in a *national* curriculum. The variousness of a living language resists being 'trammelled' by standardized prescriptions and procedures of the kind described in either the syllabuses or the National Curriculum. (In this reckoning the new insistence on spoken standard English is not a reaction against a previous liberality but the consummation of an existing tendency.) The most significant effect of the 'formulaic monotonies' was to give credence to the machinery of assessment and to discourage curiosity about its purpose. By the time HMI called for 'a national development project' on the spoken word (DES, 1986) the jargons encouraged by the concept of oracy had taken a firm hold. They were of no use in producing answers to the essential question: what kind of contribution might teachers of English be best qualified to make to the development of the spoken word if, in HMI's own words, they accept 'the claim of literature for a place at the heart of the English curriculum'? HMI offered no views. Neither had Bullock. Nor did the Cox Report (DES, 1989) on which the first Order for English was based. The consequence was that in the 1990 Order 'Speaking and Listening' was accorded the status of a separate Attainment Target and deprived of the distinctive identity it should have had as part of a specific curriculum subject – 'English': 'The development of pupils' understanding of the spoken word and the capacity to express themselves effectively in a variety of listening and speaking activities, matching style and response to audience and purpose' (DES, 1990).

The penetration of new, often unnecessary but nonetheless bemusing terminologies to the centre of English carries the risk that teachers will distrust their own intuitions and talents and hanker after irrelevant certitudes. Both Cox and the 1990 Order habitually denied the intuitive aspects of human speech and the dependence of all forms of expression, spoken or written, upon them. They gave official sanction to hitherto unimagined forms of historical and cultural amnesia. A pupil who had reached level 8 in 'Speaking and Listening' was judged ready, *en route* to level 9, to be taught that

> speech ranges from intimate or casual spontaneous conversation, *e.g. jokes, anecdotes, banter, gossip, argument*, through discussion, commentary and debate to more formal forms, such as *lectures and sermons, toasts and oaths.*
>
> (DES, 1990, p.27)

What is presented as a relatively sophisticated form of knowledge is in fact a rudimentary form of awareness that was undoubtedly possessed by our illiterate forebears – or at least by such of them as were familiar with both ale-house and church, and went both to the wedding and the feast that followed! The consequences of so spurious a conception of knowledge can be surreal: as when a researcher for the National Oracy Project calls for 'a massive research programme' to investigate (in children between five and eleven) 'areas of linguistic experience and skill...such as humour, deception, and all the indirect uses of language (irony, questions used as commands etc.)' (Norman, Ed., 1992).

One cannot help wondering what Swift or Dickens would have made of such a proposal; how they might have given us the flavour and the shape of the 'research' indicated: 'statistically significant', 'preferably longitudinal studies' of the development of humour, deception and irony, with findings to be expressed 'not just qualitatively but quantitatively'. Such portentousness is not without its own harmful effects. SEAC's publications in the early days of the 1990 Order were often marked by an alien vocabulary in which classroom teachers could not recognize themselves. Increasingly subject to centralized control, they were to envisage themselves as controllers in their turn, training their pupils to see themselves in a similarly objective way. These publications show what, in practice, Cox's definition of 'oracy' ('Oracy involves teaching and assessing children's language behaviour with other people') was to mean. One describes a group of primary school children acting out a short play. It goes well; but there are problems. There is one pupil (ten years old) who 'contributed little to the group discussion' and was 'content to participate as directed by others'; there is another who 'dominated both the planning and presenting'. This of course is normal; any classroom teacher knows it. However, for purposes of National Curriculum assessment, these pupils must be *policed*. For *'their degree of involvement was suspect and open to question* in terms of interpersonal skills and group interaction' (my italics). These pupils must be taken aside and 'in child's language' informed of the respect in which they must improve and 'how progress might be made'. In the philosophy of SEAC the human image of the teacher trusted by her pupils is obscured by that of the behavioural scientist coldly engaged in 'observation of process'. Teachers 'monitor learning behaviour' and 'check product'; they are 'assessing language behaviours rather than actual output' (SEAC, 1990).

Another SEAC publication includes an instructional video-tape for teachers assessing pupils in 'Speaking and Listening' at the end of Key Stage 1. The tape shows a trio of seven year olds in discussion. The discussion is dominated by one obviously bright and imaginative boy. His spoken English is forceful, expressive and accurate. His contributions are acknowledged (in the accompanying booklet) to be 'coherent, sustained and detailed'. However, teachers are to understand that what matters more than the verve and variety of his English is his *behaviour*. He is judged, in this little group of infants, to have 'assumed the lead role to an over dominant extent'. This is the 'weakness' of his 'performance'. He must now be asked to 'reflect on his strengths and weaknesses', to see the need to 'listen with an increased span of concentration to other children and adults, asking and responding to questions and comments on what has been said'. He must learn what his attentive listeners demonstrate: the value of 'positive body language' and 'eye contact'. In future, he is going to have 'to show greater awareness of audience' (SEAC, 1991). In this extroverted view of human relations, if you don't show you are listening, you aren't. Like the teacher in Randall Jarrell's *Pictures from an Institution* who 'listened unhearing and then flung praise over the girls with oblivious generosity', this little boy will do well to learn to look as though he is 'listening intently' even if he isn't. It is a talent that many possess but few would admit to.

To ask teachers to see their pupils in this way is gross. Its delusory advantage is that it simplifies matters. It transforms what should be questions of judgement into matters of observation. It is thus entirely consistent with the priority accorded to speech as 'language behaviour' that, in commenting on the 'Case' for the revision of National Curriculum English, SEAC should have concentrated not on questions of value but on 'problems of assessment caused by the Order's failure to define key knowledge and skills with sufficient precision'. The way ahead lay in a 'more precise definition of the essential skills' (NCC, 1992). Despite its claim to have based the 'Case' on an 'analysis of the thinking which underlies' the 1990 Order, the National Curriculum Council nowhere questioned this faith in the feasibility and value of subjecting the 'skills' of 'Speaking and Listening' to yet further definition. At one point it seemed to discern the moral implications of viewing language and its assessment in this way, only to dismiss them: English should 'promote spiritual, moral and cultural understanding. There is no conflict between these objectives and our judgement that the skills and knowledge involved would need to be defined more rigorously and explicitly' (NCC, 1992). But there *is* a conflict (as SEAC's examples show) unless that judgement is itself formed in the light of such an understanding; unless it can see what is wrong with the idea of speaking and listening as a repertoire of skills, for development by children and policing by teachers; and unless it can see what is wrong with the idea of 'progress' as it was characterized in the 1993 proposals for the revised Order. Such progress would declare itself in increasing 'fluency and confidence', 'adaptability and flexibility' and 'proficiency in different kinds of talk' (DFE, 1993). But this idea of progress can only be sustained by ignoring its implications: technical progress (the standard phrasing constantly suggests it *is* a technical matter) may be moral regress. 'Adaptability', 'flexibility' and 'proficiency' may be turned to evil as well as honourable ends. To be helped to appreciate the distinction between the two is the important thing; to present those 'skills' as self-sufficient ends is wrong. It is more important to speak honestly than to 'adapt and adjust'. When such a questionable and inadequate conception of the spoken word is enshrined in a National Curriculum the 'conflict' with the promotion of 'spiritual, moral and cultural understanding' becomes unavoidable. For a teacher who judges that a child is not cut out for 'adaptability and flexibility' is not free to act on that judgement. There are such children; there always have been:

> By nature slow of speech, I took no pleasure in conversation, nor in hearing the voices of my fellow-creatures. When people addressed me I not infrequently, especially if they were strangers, turned away my head from them, and if they persisted in their notice burst into tears, which singularity

of behaviour by no means tended to dispose people in my favour.

(Borrow, 1982, p.7)

Such children may eventually develop into good parents, and who is to say that the limits on their 'proficiency in different kinds of talk' are to be regretted when set against the proficiency of the con man, the political sophist or the smooth-talking salesman? Do we really want Borrow's modern counterparts, or indeed any children, to be confronted by the 'self-assessment prompt sheets' now appearing even in otherwise good collections of material for use in school? 'These 'prompt sheets' are intended to help you 'think about your own skills in speaking and listening': 'How much talking and listening did you do?' 'Was the balance about right?' 'Did you learn or achieve anything new?' 'What?' 'Are there any skills you need to practise more?' (Seely and Kitchen, 1995).

The idea that governs the revised Order, as it governed the old one, is not that of progress but of *progression;* not a moral but a technical idea. The kind of development delineated in this progression through levels cannot indeed be other than technical since development in the moral and expressive spheres cannot be described through hierarchies of 'skills'. The language remains mechanistic: 'Pupils are confident in matching their talk to the demands of different contexts' (SCAA, 1995). The monitoring is to go on as a distraction from the key question: what is the distinctive contribution teachers of 'English' may be expected to make in the development of the spoken word? Ironically, the new Order has given a keener edge to this question by so emphatically installing 'major works of literature' as a compulsory element. However, there is almost nothing at all in the level descriptions that marks them as belonging to 'English'. They are thus utterly without the power to inspire us with a sense of what English teachers should see as their special responsibilities towards the spoken language. We need to accept – and the next revision needs to take account of – the fact that, in so far as teachers of English may have an effect on the quality of children's spoken English, the changes will be gradual, not easily discernible and will certainly obey no rules of progression we may care to invent. Those changes, moreover, will come about through activities that may be defended as clearly belonging within 'English': through studying, savouring, discussing, reading aloud and dramatizing those forms of expression (primarily literary) that we recognize to be 'charged with eager life' (how close that phrase is to Ezra Pound's description of literature as 'language charged with meaning to the utmost degree'). It is through such activities that English teachers help children to develop a feeling for the qualities and potentialities of the English language, including their own. The hope is that the effect will show itself in their use of the language generally, whether spoken or written, and that they will develop a sense of distinction such as we must assume to have guided the teaching: a distinction between a truthful language of expressive force and a language that blurs, misleads and betrays. That they should learn to use the former and be able to discern the latter is the proper aim of English teaching.

CHAPTER SEVEN
Contemplating Literature

Contemplate: from *con* and *templum:* an open place for observation marked out by the augur with his staff.

(Oxford English Dictionary)

Dear Mr Lee

Dear Mr Lee (Mr Smart says
it's rude to call you Laurie, but that's
how I think of you, having lived with you
really all year), Dear Mr Lee
(Laurie) I just want you to know
I used to hate English, and Mr Smart
is roughly my least favourite person,
and as for Shakespeare (we're doing him too)
I think he's a national disaster, with all those jokes
that Mr Smart has to explain why they're jokes,
and even then no one thinks they're funny,
And T. Hughes and P. Larkin and that lot
in our anthology, not exactly a laugh a minute,
pretty gloomy really, so that's why
I wanted to say Dear Laurie (sorry) your book's
the one that made up for the others, if you
could see my copy you'd know it's lived
with me, stained with Coke and Kitkat
and when I had a cold, and I often
take you to bed with me to cheer me up
so Dear Laurie, I want to say sorry,
I didn't want to write a character-sketch
of your mother under headings, it seemed
wrong somehow when you'd made her so lovely,
and I didn't much like those questions
about *social welfare in the rural community*
and *the seasons as perceived by an adolescent,*
I didn't think you'd want your book
read that way, but bits of it I know by heart,

and I wish I had your uncles and your half-sisters
and lived in Slad, though Mr Smart says your view
of the class struggle is naïve, and the examiners
won't be impressed by me knowing so much by heart,
they'll be looking for terse and cogent answers
to their questions, but I'm not much good at terse and cogent,
I'd just like to be like you, not mind about being poor,
see everything bright and strange, the way you do,
and I've got the next one out of the Public Library,
about Spain, and I asked Mum about learning
to play the fiddle, but Mr Smart says Spain isn't
like that any more, it's all Timeshare villas
and Torremolinos, and how old were you
when you became a poet? (Mr Smart says for anyone
with my punctuation to consider poetry as a career
is enough to make the angels weep).

PS Dear Laurie, please don't feel guilty for
me failing the exam, it wasn't your fault,
it was mine, and Shakespeare's,
and maybe Mr Smart's, I still love *Cider,*
it hasn't made any difference.

(Fanthorpe, 1987, p.22)

'Dear Mr Lee' touches many nerves. Nobody who is professionally concerned with the teaching of literature to young people is likely to get through the poem without one or two winces. Students do indeed commonly live with prescribed texts for a whole year. But there is enforced living and real living, enforced shared accommodation on the one hand and joyful union on the other. U.A. Fanthorpe's pupil has known the latter whilst everything the teacher has done has worked to make it a mere functional matter of the former. 'Having lived with you really all year': what the living has meant becomes clear and real as the confession progresses.

What Fanthorpe delightfully reminds us of is the unpredictable messiness of our imaginative experience: messiness not in the sense of incoherence but in the sense that we come at, live in, are inspired, provoked, mesmerized, antagonized, delighted, repelled by what we read in unpredictable ways, much depending on circumstance and mood. So, *Cider with Rosie* has taken hold on this pupil's imagination via the literal messiness of everyday life. 'Live', 'lovely', 'by heart', 'bright and strange', 'love': living with the book has been an introduction to an inner world with which the child has felt in strong, instinctive sympathy. It's a confession of love, indeed, of uncritical rapture and gratitude. And no thanks to the teacher. It is too easy, Fanthorpe is telling us, to ignore (or not to feel the spirit) of the literature, to see it as the occasion for social theorizing or unfelt writing, to overlook the simple fact that, in this case, we are dealing with *children*. This child (and Laurie Lee's book) have triumphed against the odds. The child, quite against the teacher's intention, is the teacher here. What, ultimately, we think of *Cider with Rosie*; whatever the larger cultural questions it may beg or illuminate – these are irrelevant unless the book first of all seizes the imagination of the young reader. It is Quiller-Couch's point:

> it matters very little for the moment, or even for a considerable while, that a pupil does not perfectly, or even nearly, understand all he reads, provided we can get the attraction to seize upon him. He and the author between them will do the rest: our function is to communicate and trust.

> (Quiller-Couch, 1920)

It is notoriously easy to create obstacles to that attraction. We can force the pace of understanding, force-feed the mind with ideas *about* a work and with 'activities' to encourage 'active engagement' rather than, for instance, acknowledging the truthful philosophy reflected in the discredited practice of learning by heart.

'To know by heart': the very phrase enshrines a traditional wisdom about the process and nature of certain kinds of understanding. (We don't speak of learning or knowing 'by mind'.) When we commit verse or prose to memory, ordinarily we do so not for mere convenience of recall but because we acknowledge two familiar truths: firstly about the material, secondly about ourselves. The material lives in us in different ways at different times; its meaning may grow inside us the more readily if we possess it after the manner indicated by the phrase 'learning by heart'. It lies there (much like Arnold's 'touchstones') not inertly but in dynamic (or potentially dynamic) relationship with our developing experience. So that 'O Rose thou art sick' cannot, for the 'heart' to which it is committed at twenty, be the 'same' poem at forty. What may be 'bright and strange' and 'lovely' now may well change its nature as we grow older. In learning something by heart we are in a way, and paradoxically, accepting the changeability of the unchanging. The words on the page will stay the same but their meanings will change as we do. They are 'living powers' to which we can set no limits. The responsibility of the teacher of literature is, first and foremost, to give prominence to what his adult judgement tells him is most worth giving the fullest attention to: works that have the depth and the honesty to endure beyond the occasion on which we first meet them. We may not want to bring back the practice of learning by heart in any systematic way but its fall from grace is very significant of the changing view of literature and its teaching that we are living through.

Why is it out of favour? 'I still love Cider' says Fanthorpe's O level or CSE 'failure': testimony enough to the only kind of success that really matters but not, of course, either visible or interesting to examiners wanting 'terse and cogent' answers or teachers wishing to place the book in some broader ideological context. In pillorying these immediately recognizable types Fanthorpe nails the reasons for that fall from favour. Sterile examining routines have of course always been with us. Mr Smart, however, belongs to a new breed, nicely caught in 'Mr Smart says your view/of the class struggle is naïve': condescension towards the text, a superiority derived not from engaging with what is distinctive about it as art, but from hindsight about its circumstantial origins. If works of the imagination are little more than emanations from historically attestable forces and influences there obviously can't be much to be said for learning bits of them 'by heart'. For that would be to admit that the 'ideological' bonds that constrain artistic expression may be broken in the continued imaginative relationship between a work and its readers. It would be to accept that the words that we want to live with usually possess a potency beyond our immediate understanding, certainly beyond any merely historical understanding of their circumstantial origins. If our view of poems and stories is that they are interesting mainly for what we can say about their social origins and for what they can say to us about certain already determined issues or themes, then their value is exhausted once we've attended to their 'message'. ('It is widely assumed by English teachers', said James Gribble in *Literary Education: a Revaluation* (1983), one of the best books of its kind to appear in recent years, 'that literature is just a semi-fictional way of analysing moral and social problems'.) There will, moreover, be an overwhelming tendency to favour contemporary literature because it can be seen (or made to appear) to be more obviously relevant to those problems than the literature of the past. (The much resented introduction of 'canonical' authors in the 1995 Order is in one light a summary correction of this tendency.) It is clear that if literature and art are indeed no more to us than vehicles for such purposes they ought to be assimilated to the study of history, sociology or politics and forego their traditional claim to separate consideration.

It is painfully ironic to contrast the attitudes and beliefs pilloried by U.A. Fanthorpe with the wisdom of the pupil. The pupil is inarticulate, technically inept in his writing but, the key difference, *on the side of the literature*: he (or of course she) *trusts* the text and has already been sufficiently fascinated by its imaginative power to put his faith in its continuing meaning. He has submitted to its attractions. The teacher's responsibility above all is not to break its spell. Fanthorpe finds a language in which to pay a kind of wry homage to the power of the text and the natural eagerness of that child's response. In loftier language but with a kindred insight Saul Bellow speaks of the power of a work of art to 'induce a temporary suspension of activities. It leads to contemplative states, to wonderful and, to my mind, sacred states of the soul. These are not, however, passive' (Bellow, 1994). This may indeed seem an exalted language, remote in its connection with the teaching of literature. But this is Bellow's point. As he sees it, the teaching of literature has come adrift from such a language: it 'has been a disaster'; 'in colleges and universities no passion for novels and poems is instilled'. What Bellows registers is what another American critic has called 'that massive shift of focus...away from the "intrinsic" rhetorical study of literature towards study of the "extrinsic" relations of literature, its placement within psychological, historical or sociological contexts' (Miller, 1985). It is not just the 'focus' that has 'shifted'. An entire humane language of reference has moved to the margins of critical thought. Bellow – with the impregnable authority of the great practitioner – still uses it when speaking of the novel: 'you hear a voice or, more significantly, an individual tone under the words...it is more musical than verbal, and it is the characteristic signature of a person, of a soul' (Bellow, 1994). Bellow indeed consciously sustains the language of the spirit, knowing that it finds no echo in the currently predominant modes of materialist criticism and teaching.

Writers in whom we hear such a 'voice' and detect such a 'signature' have 'power over distraction and fragmentation, and out of distressing unrest, even from the edge of chaos...can bring unity and carry us into a state of intransitive attention. People hunger for this' (Bellow, 1994). In these words Bellow affirms a powerful human need, a perennial appetite, a hunger that may at one stage be fed by *Cider with Rosie*, at another by *Crime and Punishment*. Certainly they are words good for all time, and for all occasions of a teacher's professional life. Is not the power to induce 'intransitive attention' the power teachers should seek to work *with* as they seek, in Quiller-Couch's kindred words, to 'get the attraction to seize upon' their pupils? During the eighties, unfortunately, such a power was more likely to fall under suspicion than to be celebrated; to be seen (in the materialist philosophies then in the ascendant) as a form of oppression rather than (in Bellow's words again) 'a path to liberation'. There was a powerful tendency to see works of the imagination as little more than forms of conditioning, themselves conditioned by views of which we may or may not approve. 'Literature', declared one group of teachers, 'undoubtedly embodies and transmits the social-aesthetic values of white, male bourgeois society' (Batsleer *et al.*, 1985). They looked forward to a time when 'we can say that words like "culture", "politics", even "literature" with their ingrained accents of possession, separation and exclusion no longer have any meaning for us'.

This is barbarism. It has not, however, always come so ill-disguised. Terry Eagleton's clever, shallow, influential *Literary Theory* (1983) – the buoyancy of the writing so strangely at odds with its dispiriting substance – was the kind of book from which readers, including prospective teachers, were unlikely to derive anything more profitable than the sensation that literature (however defined) is in the end hardly worth their attention – that is, unless they were able to agree, as indeed many did, that the study of literature 'entails the transformation of a society divided by class and gender'. There was little room for 'passion' or the awed recognition of 'the characteristic signature of a person or a soul' in a critic who could envisage a society in which 'Shakespeare would be no more valuable than present day graffiti' or who offered 'parties' as 'texts' which can 'prove quite as rich as one of the canonical works and written dissections of [them] quite as ingenious as those of Shakespeare'.

Regular smacks of levity may make the overall triviality temporarily more palatable. It has been left to dourer voices to spell out the implications for teachers of English in the schools. Children, says a recent 'reader' for the Open University's PGCE English course (in a chapter entitled 'The Centrality of Literature'),

> must be free to make their own cultural and literary affiliations; our responsibility is to help them to a greater understanding of their own and others' choices. They need opportunities to scc texts in their full social contexts and histories, to understand the assumptions underlying both the texts and the valuations put upon them by particular groups.
>
> (Brindley, 1994, p.129)

What is a teacher to do with such advice? Of what use is it to be told that 'the heritage version of English is primarily concerned with nation building', that its 'benefits', 'whether in Newbolt or the 1990s version', are 'assumed to accrue to the dominant social order'? What can it mean to describe 'the business of English' as that of 'enabling students to develop their understanding of the way meanings are made, and of the processes whereby meanings conflict and change'? (Brindley, 1994). Such prose inhabits a self-referential world in which the phrases seem to speak not to the reader but only to each other. This is the vein in which a professor of English recently doubted the relevance of Shakespeare in schools on the grounds that his plays are part of the 'iconography of bourgeois culture' – 'they carry an élitist tag which excludes them from the legitimate business of a world defined by *Brookside* and *EastEnders*' (Holderness, 1988). A little earlier, however, the Russian poet Joseph

Brodsky, noting the anomaly of views such as this coming 'from, of all places, the local campuses', remarked that 'the application of democratic principles in the sphere of knowledge leads to equating wisdom with idiocy' (Brodsky, 1987). The moral wealth that George Eliot and her successors saw as inherent in a developed language and thus to be the component of a humane literacy becomes a source of embarrassment rather than of pride.

It was surely the absence of such pride and conviction amongst so many of those professing to represent teachers of English (the author of 'The Centrality of Literature' was Vice-Chair of the National Association for the Teaching of English) that provoked the heavy-handed and much resented intervention from the political centre during the early 1990s. The School Curriculum and Assessment Authority's English Working Group, representing 'professional judgement', wanted no prescribed names in the Reading component of the new Order and was overruled. The 'canon' is there and teachers, with or without conviction, must face up to it.

The installation of particular authors in the 1995 Order inevitably poses a number of questions. What are they there for? What, if any, do we expect their effect to be upon children's work in the other two components of National Curriculum English? If we decide what that effect should be, how do we go about achieving it? How well will undergraduate courses in English have equipped entrants to the profession to answer these questions? For the present climate of literary studies in Higher Education is, naturally, not something to which we should expect school English to remain immune. David Gervais recently regretted how seldom his

> students seem to find such things as Shakespeare's tragedies really painful. Too often they shield themselves from the immense weight of suffering in them by cool contemplation of their themes...Nor is it uncommon to find a student preferring to think about *Romeo and Juliet* in terms of an abstraction like 'Fate' rather than as a play about love.
>
> (Gervais, 1992, p.159)

Gervais relates this 'student coldness' to 'the fact that our most prominent literary critics, like Ricks and Kermode, are so much stronger in intellectual brilliance than in any emotional depth'. Students in my PGCE classes on the teaching of practical criticism regularly say how rarely they looked at poems and prose in detail during their degree courses. The emphasis was on breadth: a broad sweep across a period or genre. Inevitably they have been led to feel (though it is a feeling that does not seem to run deep) that close reading is not important in that broader understanding of literature they assume teaching it should aim to produce. There is a superficially persuasive logic to this abstention from close reading, a logic consonant with the facts of contemporary culture: the environment is awash with words and images, the two often in harness. The inexorable proliferation of artefacts – books, television programmes, newspapers, advertising copy, films, magazines – certainly induces a desire to make sense of it all, to strive for some kind of intellectual synthesis in which we shall understand their relations both with one another and within their own kind. Some such desire was reflected in the rambling comprehensiveness of the 1990 Order which made a virtue of *not* being specific in its guidance on texts (with the exception of Shakespeare). 'Attainment Target 2: reading' was defined as 'The development of the ability to read, understand and respond to all types of writing, as well as the development of information-retrieval strategies for the purposes of study' (DES, 1990). The promiscuous variety of modes and genres within which students were required to read and write reflected a binding assumption: that literacy is a matter of range of knowledge rather than depth of experience.

Under such circumstances it would have been implausible for OFSTED *not* to have reported 'a lack of balance in attention given to major aspects of English, such as the study of poetry' (OFSTED, 1995). The undiscriminating breadth of definition found in the 1990 Order worked against 'balance of attention'; indeed it tended to submerge the essential educational question – to which, in giving prominence to the study of named authors, the 1995 Order has given fresh urgency: 'What manner of thing is this collection of words before me and how may I best bring my pupils to an understanding of it?' It is troubling if unsurprising that OFSTED also reports (at Key Stages 3 and 4) 'particular weaknesses [amongst teachers] in relation to familiarity with poetry and knowledge about language' (OFSTED, 1995). Stuck with the terms and categories of its brief, OFSTED neither investigates nor comments upon the relationship between an experience of poetry and knowledge about language.

Teachers, however, need to do this. What kind of account, for instance, are we happy to give of our reasons for studying a sequence of poems (as I like to do with a Key Stage 3 class) which includes Edward Thomas's 'The Gallows', Randall Jarrell's 'Bats', Jon Silkin's 'Death of a Bird' and William Cowper's 'Epitaph on a Hare'? The range is broad: early twentieth century, modern American, contemporary English, and Augustan. I like to work in Cowper's delightful prose account (in his letters) of his tame hares, Puss, Tiney and Bess. There is a good deal of incidental work one can do on changes in English vocabulary over time, particularly in relation to the Cowper. But such work *will* be incidental. The essential quality of attention is suggested in Edward Thomas's view that 'A great writer so uses the words of everyday that they become a code of his own which the world is bound to learn and in the end take unto itself' (Thomas, 1993). Perhaps we will not nowadays think the world's compliance can be quite so readily depended upon, though with the presence of Biblical and Shakespearean idiom still active in the language we can see what Thomas meant. His statement nevertheless reminds us of what we are about. The contemplation of words naturally follows from and should deepen a sense of their mystery and their powers. (The word 'contemplation', as we see from the definition quoted at the head of this chapter, has its roots in a religious act.) The words may be of the simplest:

> ### The Gallows
>
> There was a weasel lived in the sun
> With all his family,
> Till a keeper shot him with his gun
> And hung him up on a tree,
> Where he swings in the wind and rain,
> In the sun and in the snow,
> Without pleasure, without pain,
> On the dead oak tree bough.
>
> There was a crow who was no sleeper,
> But a thief and a murderer
> Till a very late hour; and this keeper
> Made him one of the things that were,
> To hang and flap in rain and wind,
> In the sun and in the snow.
> There are no more sins to be sinned
> On the dead oak tree bough.
>
> There was a magpie, too,
> Had a long tongue and a long tail;
> He could both talk and do –
> But what did that avail?
> He, too, flaps in the wind and rain
> Alongside weasel and crow,
> Without pleasure, without pain,
> On the dead oak tree bough.
>
> And many other beasts
> And birds, skin, bone, and feather,
> Have been taken from their feasts
> And hung up there together,
> To swing and have endless leisure
> In the sun and in the snow,
> Without pain, without pleasure,
> On the dead oak tree bough.

(Thomas, 1974, p.82)

Edward Thomas's vocabulary in 'The Gallows' is simple but his theme is deep: nothing less than the nullity of death itself. Thomas harnesses what there is in the English language that invites the laconic, terse and discomforting statement and turns it to the deadening effect of his final line refrain. Weasel, crow and magpie: these are not creatures that provoke ready sympathy. So how is it that the poem awakens a kind of generalized regret for all those 'beasts/And birds, skin, bone and feather' that share the common fate? There is no sentimentality; the gamekeeper is just a part of the scheme of things. What Thomas does is to assimilate the brief, uncertain life of the animals to a sense of death in life that only we, human beings, can possess. Each stanza describes the identical route taken by (or rather forced upon) the particular animal, the narrative convention 'There was a...' enforcing the inevitability of the ignominy and finality of the death. But it is the repetition of 'without pleasure, without pain' that gives us the most direct entry into the originating feeling of 'The Gallows'. It is, read literally, simply tautological – no more than the obvious truth about death, the 'bourne from which no traveller returns'. However, the effect of that reflection is to leave us with the feeling that even pain itself is preferable to nullity, the absence of being. The dulled, unstressed, unpunctuated monosyllables are the sound of non-being; and the effect is achieved through the use of some of the most solid of English words. This is perhaps the most arresting feature of the poem; that Thomas works with an elemental language that is also the language of the elements: wind and rain, sun and snow are the elements in which the animals swing, hang and flap. It is a rudimentary language for a rudimentary existence.

There is in fact a touch of the anthropomorphic in 'The Gallows': the weasel 'with all his family', the crow 'a thief and a murderer'. But this is no more than to suggest the deep connections between the animal and human worlds: the keeper, like the poet, like his readers, must eventually be 'without pain, without pleasure'. Those deep connections are at one level symbolized in the common language: we inhabit a natural world in which, for all the changes wrought by time and for all the variety of our material circumstances, the elemental facts are pretty well unchanged; for those facts no one has produced words more useful than the old ones. Weather-forecasters may speak of 'precipitation' but 'snowfall' is the word we carry on with as our own. Through the old, elemental words Thomas draws us into a meditation on truths that have changed as little as they have.

Of course that meditation will not, with children, be of the kind that I am drawing out here, but in sharing Thomas's words with them we will be deepening their sense of how those words may be used to explore important matters. We will be helping them towards that inwardness with language that is a matter of feeling (rather than knowing) the vital part it plays in our sense of identity and connection. Thomas depends upon our intuitive grasp of this fact; if it were not a fact his poem would itself be 'dead' on the bough of English! And here we see how the *understanding* of literature and the question of how far we should go in trying to establish and deepen it calls for tact: a tact that cannot be acquired as a 'skill' but will be developed only through experience of literature. A good teacher with know how far to press pupils towards the explicitness of connection between the animal and the human world. It may not be very far at all. Many will now need to be told what a gallows is. There are some obvious questions that may be asked so as to focus the poem. Where is the scene set? What do the creatures have in common? What does the keeper feel about them? What does the writer feel about them? But the vital requirement is that the poem be savoured for what it is: that its diction, its form and its rhythms are felt in performance. Maybe here it will be the teacher's performance that will communicate the solid strength of the diction, the sense of an old story being replayed, the dulled resignation of the refrain. Or these things may be discovered in rehearsed readings. However the lesson is organized it should take place in a continuous programme of teaching shaped by one very clearly understood principle: the words it seeks to put before the young should answer to Edward Thomas's own description of them as 'strange as the races/Of dead and unborn' and 'yet worn new again and again'. For what is strange about words (in Thomas's view) is what cannot be fathomed, what we take on trust as an inheritance bred with the blood and bone. This suggests, as the particular province of 'English', that we are dealing with a quality of language we know to be both rooted in an inconceivable past and capable of endless renewal as we call upon it to serve our present needs. To lose our apprehension of its strangeness (a quality to command our respect and sensitivity in our use of the language) is to risk abusing it and severing those connections that make for its continued health.

The language of Edward Thomas's poetry is surely language 'charged with meaning to the utmost possible degree'. The 'familiarity with poetry' which the OFSTED inspectors demand in teachers needs to be more than a knowledge of what is available or prescribed. It needs to include a recognition (so clearly registered by Newbolt in its remarks on the inextricability of 'knowledge of English' and knowledge of literature) that truly to contemplate and inhabit language so charged will have its due effect upon our own use of English, spoken as well as written. Only with the kind of feeling for language that we recognize as the mark of great and good writers are we likely to produce good writing ourselves. We need first to experience that feeling as it embodies itself in poems, stories and plays. What are the methods by which we are most likely to bring about such an experience? Which are most likely to obstruct it? We can state it as an axiom that unless we believe (and are able to engender the beginnings of a similar belief amongst our pupils) in Pound's words we shouldn't be bothering with literature at all – and we shouldn't be surprised when our pupils' writing fails to improve. Such a belief cannot of course be implanted by curricular directive. Prescription cannot guarantee good teaching; it cannot legislate for the appropriate attitude and depth of understanding amongst teachers.

Prescription comes at a time when, for the majority of English teachers, the object of literature teaching is probably more accurately reflected in the 1995 Order's statement that 'the main emphasis should be on the encouragement of wider reading in order to develop independent, responsive and enthusiastic readers' than upon the accompanying statement that some texts should be 'studied in detail' (DES, 1995).[1] To be independent and responsive is to have achieved high and proper aims; it is to have become a critical reader. What the Order implies here is that it is somehow possible to become such a reader without 'detailed study', an impression confirmed in the statement that 'Pupils should be encouraged to appreciate the distinctive qualities of these works through activities that emphasize the interest and pleasure of reading them, rather than necessitating a detailed, line-by-line study' (DES, 1995). It is of course easy to understand and sympathize with the rejection of 'line-by-line study': some of the worst and laziest pedantries implied in the phrase have been abundantly documented over the years. (Ironically, the Order positively encourages these pedantries in its quaintly anachronistic insistence that 'pupils should be taught...to extract meaning beyond the literal' and 'analyse and discuss hidden meanings'.) And yet the opposition between 'detailed study' and 'interest and pleasure' is false: such study may be the only way in which interest can be aroused – at least in so far as it is an interest in the 'distinctive qualities' of the work. Is it possible to understand such qualities in the work of, say, Donne, Marvell, Milton or Pope (all amongst the prescribed range of poets) without close study? These are all no doubt authors whose work, it is supposed, will 'extend pupils' ideas and their moral and emotional understanding' (DES, 1995). And so they should, properly taught. And yet, if the method is bad, no prescription will be of any value.

---

[1] The publishers' lists are impressive proof of the wealth that such encouragement can now call on. One thinks of Heinemann's African and Caribbean Writers series; of the 'Figures in a Landscape' series (Cambridge University Press) with writing from Australia, Canada, India, Ireland and South Africa; and of the healthy competition to produce good editions of Shakespeare for schools.

Method, of course, is inconceivable outside the context of the ideas that shape it. Those ideas may support and, equally, they may hinder or altogether prevent that 'moral and emotional understanding'. In recent years we have seen a proliferation of commercial materials that have had their eye primarily upon the generation of 'interest and pleasure' and on the encouragement of 'response', but with only the most oblique of bearings upon such understanding. Frequently they have exhibited what Jonathan Sacks calls the 'fallacy of modernity' which produces 'a world of individuals as makers of their own meanings'. Sacks say of 'moral education' that

> It is becoming part of a community with a particular tradition, history and way of life. It is like learning a language. The contradiction at the heart of individualism is that there can be a self unencumbered by tradition, unfettered in its freedom. That is as inconceivable as an art without conventions or a thought without a language in which it can be expressed. The sovereign self, by dissolving its attachments, has become a kingdom without a country.

(Sacks, 1991, p.44)

This has its immediate bearing upon teaching method, as it does upon the reasons why we should give priority to literature written in English over 'texts from other cultures and traditions'. What, for instance, does it take to read Edward Thomas's First World War poem 'As The Team's Head-Brass' (reproduced in a recent teaching anthology)? For a start (if you are a student), it helps if you read other poems by Edward Thomas (such as 'The Gallows'); if you have some familiarity with those undeclarative tones; if you have begun to find them lingering in the imagination when more public voices are forgotten. You may then more readily feel your way into 'As the Team's Head-Brass'. Like so much of Thomas's verse it draws the reader into its outwardly uneventful narrative almost, apparently, idly. It has the ruminative feel of unhurried gossip. Indeed that is partly what it records: intermittently, as the ploughman goes about his work, he and the speaker exchange observations about the war:

> One of my mates is dead. The second day
> In France they killed him. It was back in March,
> The very night of the blizzard, too.

That blizzard had felled the elm on which the speaker sits:

> As the team's head-brass flashed out on the turn
> The lovers disappeared into the wood.
> I sat among the boughs of the fallen elm
> That strewed the angle of the fallow, and
> Watched the plough narrowing a yellow square
> Of charlock.

To say that the human catastrophe is paralleled by the fallen elm would be to reduce the poem to a diagram. It is not that. Thomas is the least didactic of poets. The poem finishes, as the conversation comes to an end, with an immemorial image:

> Then
> The lovers came out of the wood again:
> The horses started and for the last time
> I watched the clods crumble and topple over
> After the ploughshare and the stumbling team.

(Thomas, 1974, p.29)

It is extraordinarily sophisticated writing. It assumes sympathetic imagination in the reader. It makes no concessions to impatience or to unfamiliarity with the contemplative mode that was Thomas's instinct. It evokes a community with 'a particular tradition, history and way of life' and it communicates Thomas's love for and affinity with it. The tradition for Thomas was carried vitally through words, ordinary words 'strange as the races/Of dead and unborn' and 'Yet worn again and again'. To read Thomas is to understand what he meant by 'a language not to be betrayed'. Thomas of course was not writing for adolescents. The anthologists are. So the approaches are 'as active as possible, so that readers examine meanings in many different ways'. These 'have been designed to lead students through a process of making meaning': 'Make a sketch or diagram of the scene in the poem, showing the field, the tree, the wood, the characters, the movement of the ploughing team and so on' (Torbe and Fry, 1990). Techniques suitable for reporting on a road accident. The power of Thomas's poem would not be what it is if we were primarily aware of its cartography. The words will have their effect if we trust them, as Thomas trusted them. To schematize the scene Thomas describes is to weaken the current of feeling it should awaken in the reader: the feeling that this scene embraces immemorial tragedy and the certitude of renewal. It is to weaken the words of the poet and the hold of the reader upon them. One is reminded of the common effect of television pictures on the words they accompany: pictures only obliquely or co-incidentally relevant to what is being said crowd out meaning. We find it more, not less, difficult to attend to the words. We are not to be trusted to listen; we need (it is assumed) a pictorial mediator who, too often, weakens our grasp on events and their meaning.

With any text we have judged worthy of close study, the primary concern should not be that we 'make our own meanings' but that we open ourselves to those created by its author. Too often, the effect of designing methods 'to lead students through a process of making meaning' is to lead them away from the work itself. This road leads not to inwardness with the language – the author's and thus (this being English) our own – but into distraction and triviality. What are we doing to Marvell's 'To his Coy Mistress'; what are we doing for students' understanding of its enduring power; what are we teaching them about the possibilities of language in the hands of the greatest writers if we follow the approach recommended in one recent publication on the teaching of poetry? (Bleiman, 1995). This approach involves one pupil reading the poem aloud and another 'answering back' – 'a way of becoming involved in persuasive techniques and gaining experience of being the subject of them'. Thus, having listened to the opening two lines:

> Had we but world enough, and time,
> This coyness, lady, were no crime.

the respondent should 'interrupt, with any comments or arguments of his/her own e.g. "you might like to think I'm being coy but frankly I just don't fancy you. Your ego's so enormous that you think you're irresistible to all women"'. Marvell's images of time and eternity:

> But at my back I always hear
> Time's winged chariot hurrying near:
> And yonder all before us lie
> Deserts of vast eternity.

are mere 'strategies used by the speaker to argue his viewpoint'. Such crassness, as has been well said, 'panders to the unwillingness of many pupils to attend carefully to what someone else is saying, weighing it and evaluating it rather than polishing soundbites' (Dean, 1995). It is an approach that exhibits in its purest form the dissociation of 'oral skills' ('techniques' and 'strategies') from matters of content and value.

That 'approaches are as active as possible' is far from being the virtue assumed. That depends on the activity. Students may be very 'actively' prevented from engaging with the 'literature of high quality' prescribed in the 1995 Order. One typical and widely used compilation of materials, faithfully reflecting the orthodoxy in which *any* response to a work of literature is valid as a 'making of meaning', makes a point of being full of 'Action' – a key-word in its complex plans for 'tackling' texts (*Great Expectations, Animal Farm, Brighton Rock, The Crucible,* etc.) and bringing them to heel. The means are to hand: a variety of instruments smacking of the laboratory rather than the study – time-charts, line graphs, bar-graphs, spider diagrams, target charts, ripple charts, pie-charts and stepping charts. Those books – disturbing, refractory, exhilarating creatures, sprung from highly individual imaginations – can thus all be, literally, brought into line. Alternatively, they may be gentled into quiescence, deprived of their sting by the soft touch of party games. There is an all-purpose package of these called 'Nine Ideas for Any Text'. We can put the characters on trial, write their obituaries, invent coats of arms for their families, make them the subject of 'parcel games' or speculate on what each might keep in a personal 'treasure chest'. This is literature for the age of technology; indeed literature *as* technology.

The individual books hardly seem to matter; they become the arbitrary occasion for the games and the gimmickry. The teacher is transformed into something between a master of ceremonies and a factory foreman. He'll be overseeing the design of a coat of arms for Lady Bracknell or acting as quality controller in the production of drawings for replicas of Dickens' characters. He'll be checking 'target charts' reflecting the 'levels of commonsense' reached by the characters in Stan Barstow's *Joby,* or he'll be ponderings bar-graphs showing the levels of power different characters exercise over the poor boy. Or he'll be scrutinizing maps of Joby's home town, before assigning the student draughtsman the plum job of converting the whole novel into a board game – not difficult perhaps if his teacher has already managed to show him how 'the ideas and events of *The Importance of Being Earnest*' might be represented in a board game 'along the lines of snakes and ladders' (Little *et al.*, 1989). The effect of such apparatus, supposedly applicable to all books, is to homogenize them, to iron away the recalcitrant angles and edges of a book's individuality, to resolve the magnificent diversity of different texts into a set of mathematical equivalencies where the creative functions of language are irrelevant.

The technical paraphernalia is a substitute for real study, for intelligence and for the quality of attention to language that good literature demands. (The same publisher's *Focus on Fiction* (Saunders *et al.*, 1994), however, shows what can be done when the books are approached through activities based on careful, discriminating understanding.) What matters is not literature but what can be done to it or with it. Indeed, language itself is implicitly regarded as a flawed medium: inherently imprecise, hardly accessible without the provision of visual support. Whether it's John Steinbeck, Graham Greene, Arthur Miller or Dickens, none escapes the general implication that his work will be better understood if students are captioning cartoons, creating caricatures or using the kit provided to contrive faces for his characters. This is a common delusion, often contaminating even the saner material currently being produced for schools. We don't need pictures to see what an author means. The precisions of literary portraiture cannot be reproduced pictorially. The 1995 Order says that pupils should 'be given opportunities to...consider how texts are changed when adapted to different media, *e.g. the original text of a Shakespeare play and televised or film versions'* (DES, 1995). To do that (a very demanding undertaking) requires a much more sophisticated sense of the relationship between words and images than is reflected in most of the currently available material. 'Head your account' (of a character from *Great Expectations*) 'with a drawing of their face'. You are provided with a kit, called 'Making Faces' (Little *et al.*, 1989).

It is misleading, says Jonathan Miller, to think of description and depiction as 'interchangable modes of representation'. Hardy's Tess or Jane Austen's Mr Darcy 'are made of the same materials as the novels in which they occur, and they cannot be liberated in order to make a personal appearance in another medium':

> In *Great Expectations*, Dickens describes Mr Wemmick as having a mouth like a letter-box, and he re-inforces the comparison by insisting that the clerk posts his food as opposed to eating it. The mind's eye appears to have no difficulty in conjuring up a mouth that conforms to this description, but there is no way a picture could express such a comparison.

> (Miller, 1986, p.226)

Miller's observations are those of a perceptive critic whose sensitivity to the distinctive character of different media has been sharpened by his work in film, opera and television. He knows what literature is and what it is not: 'What is so valuable and memorably peculiar about Mr Carker, with his teeth and his wickedness, is the fact that he is in *Dombey and Son* and cannot get out' (Miller, 1986).

Much current practice works to blunt that memorable peculiarity. In the face of the diagrammatic paraphernalia, the traditional image of the teacher with book in hand, carefully reading and discussing with her pupils what they together understand and respond to on the page, no doubt seems intolerably modest. And yet without it what becomes of the teaching of literature? The Canadian critic Roger Shattuck has addressed the question with great astuteness and insight. His immediate focus is the teaching of literature in universities; however, 'How to Rescue Literature', a chapter in his book *The Innocent Eye* (1984), has equal relevance to literature as it is taught in schools. (I find it indispensable in my own teaching.) Shattuck prepares the way for his principal recommendations with two cameos of teachers with fundamentally different views of their responsibilities. On the one hand there is the elderly professor whose seminars on Cervantes consist largely of his reading the text aloud with a 'running commentary on the language, historical background and cross-references in the novel'. On the other hand there is the intense and ambitious assistant professor whose interpretation of a text involves covering the blackboard with carefully lettered diagrams, assorted symbols and equations. This professor is the author of 'two stunning articles combining communications theory and speech-act theory in an analysis of comic strips'. He is strongly fancied for promotion. The Cervantes professor, on the contrary, is considered by some faculty members to be the scandal of the Spanish department.

Shattuck's irony lies very lightly over this opposition between ancient and modern but his drift is clear enough. In that university, at least, and in much of the higher education he takes it to represent, the teaching of literature has parted company with the commitment and the love from which it should derive. The young professor, in his preference for diagrammatical analysis over performance and his attachment to contemporary trivia rather than classic texts, represents the arrogation of the teacher above his material. The commitment is to explaining it rather than drawing his students into it. The old man's commitment is precisely the opposite. Little given to explication and interpretation, he is nonetheless a teacher of literature in a tradition that Shattuck evokes in describing his 'expressive and very clear voice. His histrionic gestures and shifts in emphasis played constantly between the comic and the passionate'. It was performance with a purpose: 'At frequent intervals a student would read from his own text – haltingly yet catching some of the professor's feeling and even a few of his gestures'. Shattuck notes 'the deep-seated reluctance of most literature teachers to read aloud, to interpret orally' and is with Henry James in holding that (in James's words) 'the essential property of such a form [i.e. literature] is to give out its finest and most numerous secrets, and to give them out most gratefully, under the closest pressure – which is of course the pressure of the attention articulately sounded' (James, 1934). Shattuck's key recommendation follows:

> I wish to suggest that the critical activity of teaching literature should include as one of its essential goals the *oral* interpretation of literary texts. At least for literary criticism as it is practised in the classroom and lecture hall, the acid test is not the intellectual brilliance of the teacher's argument but the demonstrability of the interpretation when he (or someone else) actually reads aloud a sizeable passage. I will not maintain that every literary effect will be clear in an oral interpretation. But the continuous challenge of recitation keeps us alert to gesture and tone of voice, and to the burden of the argument and figurative language which they weave together.
> (Shattuck, 1984, p.320)

This was Alfred North Whitehead's view too. In contending that 'above all the art of reading aloud should be cultivated' he addressed the implications directly to teachers:

> I lay it down as an educational axiom that in teaching you will come to grief

as soon as you forget that your pupils have bodies...The connections between intellectual activity and the body, though diffused in every bodily feeling, are focused in the eyes, the ears, the voice and the hands.

(Whitehead, 1967, p.50)

Dylan Thomas was evidently of the same mind when he said that 'the voice discovers the poet's ear'. It may be that, because most of our reading is done silently, our capacities to make such discoveries tend to atrophy. C.S. Lewis thought so. He had no doubt that it was possible to be both 'highly educated' and grossly insensitive to the music of words:

They have no ears. They read exclusively by eye. The most horrible cacophonies and the most perfect specimens of rhythm and vocalic melody are to them exactly equal. It is by this that we discover some highly educated people to be unliterary. They will write 'the relation between mechanisation and nationalisation' without turning a hair.

(Lewis, 1992, p.29)

In no doubt deliberate overstatement, Robert Frost described 'the eye reader' as 'a barbarian'. He wasn't thinking purely of the reader of poetry. He would have agreed with C.S. Lewis:

Because good words can thus compel, thus guide us into every cranny of a character's mind or make palpable and individual Dante's Hell or Pindar's gods'-eye view of an island, good reading is always aural as well as visual. For the sound is not merely a superadded pleasure, though it may be that too, but part of the compulsion; in that sense, part of the meaning. This is true even of a good, working prose.

(Lewis, 1992, p.90)

If we find any truth in these united views we can't fail to be astonished that the authors of a widely used collection of materials to support oral work in 'English' dismiss reading aloud in these terms: 'The occasions when reading aloud has a real communicative purpose are nowadays very limited...Training for the "public" uses of reading aloud (public address system announcements, broadcasting, lessons in church, etc.) is best left to the relevant institutions' (Brooks *et al.*, 1986). At a stroke this dismisses a mode of learning, the voicing of imaginative language, that (like drama) belongs fundamentally within 'English'. It conceives of 'training' in an entirely external way. It ignores the possibilities Shattuck outlines when he remarks that 'A large part of religious training and military disciplines is based on the ancient belief that by learning and performing the outward physical emotions and moral attitudes we will come to experience those emotions and attitudes inwardly'. Such a belief smacks of indoctrination and might seem to have little to offer. However, the clue to the usefulness of the principle is given in Shattuck's next sentence: 'Training the voice in control and expressiveness very probably enlarges the scope of mental states available to us – particularly in a culture where the tonalities of speech have fallen badly into neglect and abuse'. I guess that Shattuck's remark about the abuse of speech refers both to quality and quantity. It is impossible for most of us to escape the deluge of words that daily pours through and from the aural media. Never before have so many words been *heard*, so few *listened* to. The frantic patter of the disc jockey is symbolic here. The content is usually negligible or inane, the volume and intensity are frequently high, and the overall impression is that there are actually no real listeners, no one to whom anything that's said actually matters. The less the significance, the greater the noise.

Shattuck concludes his 'How to Rescue Literature' by remarking that 'those of us who deal with language and literature can do far more than we are doing to keep the spoken word alive and responsive to its expressive resources'. This is certainly true in British schools. Reading aloud is undoubtedly a depressed and undeveloped area of English teaching. Generations of children have suffered and continue to suffer the dreary routines of reading aloud around the class: reading usually unrehearsed, often deadening the text and boring the captive audience. In many schools that is all reading aloud amounts to, though it need not be so. There are good resources available (Newbould and Stibbs, 1983), though not nearly enough; but there is as yet an insufficiently developed understanding that, properly done, reading aloud – performance – is the nearest we are likely to get to what Shattuck calls 'an integrated process of reading', one that 'keeps in touch with the whole of our being, mind and body, reason and feeling'. Here lies the special responsibility of English teachers in the matter of speaking and listening – one that leaves no mark whatever in the relevant 'level descriptions' of the 1995 Order. Shakespeare (and most particularly Shakespeare in performance) provides the most obvious testing ground for this perception; but the inclusiveness of Shattuck's definition suggests what we *should* mean in speaking of 'the centrality of literature' in the teaching of English. Under 'the pressure of the attention articulately sounded', there is no work of literature that will not 'give out' its 'secrets' more readily than if read in silence.

Take, for instance, John Wain's 'Au Jardin des Plantes', a poem immediately appealing and accessible to adolescents. Questions of 'being', of 'mind and body, reason and feeling' are its very theme. The poem itself is a way of enabling us to keep in touch with the meaning of those questions. A classroom approach based on such an understanding can be a richer experience than one could guess from anything the 1995 Order has to say about reading and literature (it has *nothing* to say about reading aloud after Key Stage 2).

Au Jardin des Plantes

The gorilla lay on his back,
One hand cupped under his head,
Like a man.

Like a labouring man tired with work,
A strong man with his strength burnt away
In the toiling of earning a living.

Only of course he was not tired out with work,
Merely with boredom; his terrible strength
All burnt away by prodigal idleness.

A thousand days, and then a thousand days,
Idleness licked away his beautiful strength
He having no need to earn a living.

It was all laid on, free of charge.
We maintained him, not for doing anything,
But for being what he was.

And so that Sunday morning he lay on his back,
Like a man, like a worn-out man,
One hand cupped under his terrible hard head.

Like a man, like a man,
One of those we maintain, not for doing anything,
But for being what they are.

A thousand days, and then a thousand days,
With everything laid on, free of charge,
They cup their heads in prodigal idleness.

(Poole and Shepherd, 1972, p.58)

It is a poem that presents obvious temptations. It is obviously a gift to collectors of thematic material on animals, to a teacher who wants to start a debate about zoos, about attitudes towards the natural world or about various kinds of exploitation. The temptation is increased by the brevity. All those issues can be extrapolated, and quickly. However, what matters is not that we can show the poem as touching upon the issues but that it should be experienced for what it is. It is not a tract, its purpose is not didactic. It is one of those poems that should trouble us not simply because of its ostensible theme (we can't deny its moral content) but because it is formally very beguiling: there is pleasure in its play with words, in the carefully judged repetitions and deliberately laboured rhythms. It's to this play that a good reading aloud will do justice; it will respond to the unmistakable power of the poem's ordering to evoke both the interminable sameness of the gorilla's life and the correspondingly weary acceptance that this dreadful state of affairs is of our own making. Tone is important here: there is more than one voice in the poem. There is the almost flip quality, the offhandedness of the casual phrases: 'It was all laid on, free of charge'; there is the stern impersonality, the Biblical tones of 'his terrible strength all burnt away by prodigal idleness'; there is the deliberate, savouring meditation on the meaninglessness to which the beast has been condemned: 'a thousand days, and then a thousand days' – all coming together in the collected repetitions of the last stanza. The final effect is of dissociation; these voices do not belong together. Nature seems divided against itself if it can accommodate these disparate tones. And yet we *do* accommodate them; we know as speakers of idiomatic English where each of these voices originates. The art of reading aloud is to listen for the varied cadences of the idioms upon which the poem draws and, in voicing them, to give them their proper value.

What will this mean in practice? It will mean recognizing and duly stressing the sharp little words 'cup' and 'cupped' (so human a gesture, so inapposite for a creature of such natural majesty). It will mean delivering the line 'In the toiling of earning a living' with the dulled stresses of the repeated participles: this is not a human being we are surveying but the effect of the gorilla's captivity is to suggest that little now divides him from an exhausted man. It will mean giving the called-for weight to the key words 'terrible', 'prodigal' and 'beautiful', each one of which, in its signification of concentrated gifts or power, is felt to belong to a quality of being from which the creature has been excluded. It will mean registering the stress upon 'doing' and 'being', perhaps with the slightest of ironic inflections in the latter word since it is the creature's being that is denied – trapped, suffocated, ruined. A good reading aloud, in other words, will work with the poem, will allow itself to be instructed by the ordering, the rational balance previously detected.

If we work in this way, we work in creative collaboration both with the language of the poem and the language of the reader. For indeed it is a shared language; what we are trying to do is to deepen the sharing, to strengthen the feeling for words as the carriers of fresh and invigorating meaning. To speak of feeling in this way is to imply a regular feature of work of this kind: that the educated, sensitive and experienced powers of the adult reader will bring out the life that is within the words better than the inexperienced eye. This is the way to deepen respect for words and for language more generally. An old-style comprehension approach might ask what the poet means by 'terrible strength' and 'beautiful strength' ('say in your own words'); read well, 'Au Jardin des Plantes' will create a context of feeling within which those key words can be brought explicitly into focus. It is quality of attention to words and meanings that concerns us.

No dictionary definition of 'terrible' and 'beautiful' will get us very far; nor will a rehearsal of contemporary usage – both words are devalued in ways too obvious to need expounding. What we need is to contemplate their deeper, their historical significations.

Here is an opportunity to explore the roots of the word 'terrible', to disclose its association with the awe-inspiring and mysterious as well as its connections with 'terror' (a word that retains much of its old strength); perhaps to quote *Henry V*:

> Then imitate the action of the tiger;
> Stiffen the sinews, summon up the blood,
> Disguise fair nature with hard-favour'd rage;
> Then lend the eye a terrible aspect;

or part 2 of *Henry IV*:

> I would my name were not so terrible to the enemy as it is

or the 'Song of Solomon':

> Who is she that looketh forth as the morning, fair as the moon, clear as the sun, and terrible as an army with banners?

Yeats' 'a terrible beauty is born' of course makes the connection between Wain's two key words (I imagine this is a deliberate echo). 'Beauty' is perhaps the more easily discussed: it stands out from the poem more than any other word, so removed is its meaning from the norm. More even than 'terrible', 'beauty' and 'beautiful' have been emptied of their inner meaning, their application to anything other than material objects. Shakespeare's lines from *Twelfth Night* are startling for their discordance with modern usage:

> O! What a deal of scorn looks beautiful
> In the contempt and anger of his lip.

as are these lines from 'Isaiah':

> How beautiful upon the mountains are the feet of him that bringeth good tidings, that publisheth peace.

This is the natural work of English teaching: to deepen awareness of the roots and changing force of the language, to demonstrate and thus to develop habits of attention proper to language used well or badly. Reading aloud (whether by teacher or pupil), properly rehearsed, necessitates such attention. What we are concerned with is 'the integral process of reading' of which, as we see, speaking and listening are a vital part. Much of our everyday reading is a kind of looking through words or, as indeed we say, a looking over them; much of it demands no more. But reading such as we are considering here requires that we look at and look within the words, weigh them in their relations to what surrounds them, feel ourselves into their character and quality. To do that, habitually, is to get to know our native language at a depth and in a subtlety of relation to our powers of thought and feeling that no abstract 'knowledge about language' can possibly equal.

References

Arnold, M. (1873) *Literature and Dogma*, London: Nelson.

Austen, J. (1953) *Mansfield Park*, London: Collins.

Austen, J. (1902) *Sense and Sensibility*, London: Macmillan.

Baldick, C. (1983) *The Social Mission of English Criticism, 1848–1932*, Oxford: OUP.

Batsleer, J., Davies, T., O'Rourke, R. and Weedon, C. (1985) *Rewriting English: Cultural Politics of Gender and Class*, London: Methuen.

Bellow, S. (1994) *It All Adds Up*, London: Secker and Warburg.

Beynon, J., Doyle, B., Goulden, H. and Hartley, J. (1983) 'The politics of discrimination: media studies in English teaching', *English in Education*, 17/3, 3–14.

Blake, W. (1972) *Complete Writings*, Oxford: OUP.

Bleiman, B. (1995) *The Poetry Pack: Exploring Poems at GCSE and A Level*, London: English and Media Centre.

Borrow, G. (1982) *Lavengro*, Oxford: OUP.

Brindley, S. (ed.) (1994) *Teaching English*, London: Routledge/Open University.

Britton, J. (1975) *Language and Learning*, London: Penguin.

Brodsky, J. (1987) *Less Than One*, London: Penguin.

Brooks, G., Foxman, D. and Gorman, T. (1995) *Standards in Literacy and Numeracy: 1945–1995*, London: National Commission for Education.

Brooks, G., Latham, A. and Rex, J. (1986) *Developing Oral Skills*, London: Heinemann.

Calvino, I. (1987) *The Literature Machine*, London: Secker and Warburg.

Carroll, L. *The Complete Works of Lewis Carroll*, London: The Nonesuch Press.

Carter, R. (ed.) (1991) *Knowledge about Language and the Curriculum: the LINC Reader*, London: Hodder and Stoughton.

Carter, R. and Burton, D. (Eds) (1982) *Literary Text and Language Study*, London: Arnold.

Coleridge, S. T. (1972) *On the Constitution of the Church and State*, London: Dent.

Coleridge, S.T. *Aids to Reflection*, London: George Routledge and Sons.

Cosmopolitan (February 1985 and May 1995), London.

Cox, B. (1991) *Cox on Cox: an English curriculum for the 90s*, London: Hodder and Stoughton.

138

Dean, P. (1995) review in *The Use of English*, **47** (1).

Dixon, J. (1975) *Growth through English – set in the perspective of the seventies*, Oxford: NATE and OUP.

Doughty, P. (1974) *Language, English and the Curriculum*, London: Arnold.

Eagleton, T. (1983) *Literary Theory: an Introduction*, Oxford: Blackwell.

Education and Science, Dept for (1993) *English for ages 5 to 16 (1993): proposals of the Secretary of State for Education and the Secretary of State for Wales*, London: HMSO.

Education and Science, Dept for (1993a) *Key Stage 3 English Anthology*, London: SEAC.

Education and Science, Dept for (1995) *English in the National Curriculum*, London: HMSO.

Education and Science, Dept of (1975) *A Language for Life* (Bullock Report), London: HMSO.

Education and Science, Dept of (1984) *English from 5 to 16: Curriculum Matters 1*, an HMI Series, London: HMSO.

Education and Science, Dept of (1986) *English from 5 to 16: The Responses to Curriculum Matters 1*, an HMI Report, London: HMSO.

Education and Science, Dept of (1987) *The National Curriculum 5–16*, a *consultation document*, London: HMSO.

Education and Science, Dept of (1988) *Report of the Committee of Inquiry Into The Teaching of English Language* (Kingman Report), London: HMSO.

Education and Science, Dept of (1989) *English for Ages 5 to 16*: Proposals of the Secretary of State for Education and the Secretary of State for Wales (Cox Report), London: HMSO.

Education and Science, Dept of (1990) *English in the National Curriculum*, London: HMSO.

Eggar, T. (1991) *Times Educational Supplement*, 28 June 1991.

Eliot, G. (1922) *Adam Bede*, Oxford: OUP.

Eliot, G. (1990) *Selected Essays, Poems and other Writings*, London: Penguin.

Eliot, T.S. (1959) *Four Quartets*, London: Faber and Faber.

Enright, D.J. (1981) *Collected Poems*, Oxford: OUP.

Evans, C. (1993) *English People – The Experience of Teaching and Learning English in British Universities*, Buckingham: Open University Press.

Evans, G. (1970) *Where Beards Wag All: the relevance of the oral tradition*, London: Faber and Faber.

Fanthorpe, U. (1987) *A Watching Brief*, Calstock, Cornwall: Peterloo Books.

Gervais, D. (1992) 'Literary Criticism and the Literary Student', *English*, **41**, number 170, 149–161.

Greenbaum, S. (Ed.) (1985) *The English Language Today*, Oxford: Pergamon.

Gribble, J. (1983) *Literary Education: a Revaluation*, Cambridge: CUP.

Haight, G. (1985) *Selections from George Eliot's Letters*, London: Yale University Press

Harrison, T. (1987) *Selected Poems*, London: Penguin.

Havel, V. (1991) *Open Letters*, London: Faber and Faber.

Heaney, S. (1988) *Preoccupations: Selected Prose 1968–1978*, London: Faber and Faber.

HMI (1986) *Teaching Poetry in the Secondary School – an HMI view*, London: HMSO.

HMSO (1921) *The Teaching of English in England* (Newbolt Report), London: HMSO.

HMSO (1985) *The Development of Higher Education into the 1990s*, London: HMSO.

Holbrook, D. (1961) *English for Maturity*, Cambridge: CUP.

Holbrook, D. (1979) *English for Meaning*, Windsor: National Foundation for Educational Research.

Holderness, G. (ed.) (1988) *The Shakespeare Myth*, Manchester: Manchester University Press.

Hughes, T. (1967) *Poetry in the Making*, London: Faber and Faber.

Hughes, T. (1994) *Winter Pollen*, London: Faber and Faber.

Ishiguro, K. (1989) *The Remains of the Day*, London: Faber and Faber.

James, H. (1934) *The Art of the Novel*, New York: Scribner.

Jarrell, R. (1987) *Pictures from an Institution*, London: Faber and Faber.

Jesperson, O. (1922) *Progress in Language*.

Johnson, S. (1755) *A Dictionary of the English Language*.

Jones. M. and West. A. (1988) *Learning Me Your Language*, London: Mary Glasgow Publications.

Lawrence, D.H. (1958) *The Rainbow*, London: Penguin.

Lawrence, D.H. (1960) *Lady Chatterley's Lover*, London: Penguin.

Lawrence, D.H. (1961) *Phoenix*, London: Heinemann.

Le Guin, U. (1989) *The Language of the Night*, London: The Women's Press.

Leavis, F.R. (1933) *For Continuity*, London: Chatto and Windus.

Leavis, F.R. (1962) *Two Cultures: the Significance of C.P. Snow*, Cambridge: CUP.

Leavis, F.R. (1969) *English Literature in Our Time and the University*, Cambridge: CUP.

Leavis, F.R. (1972) *Nor Shall My Sword*, London: Chatto and Windus.

Leavis, F.R. and Thompson, D. (1933) *Culture and Environment*, London: Chatto and Windus.

Levi, P. (1958) *Se Questo è un Uomo*, Torino: Einaudi. *If This is a Man*, (1995) London: Abacus.

Levi, P. (1963) *La Tregua*, Torino: Einaudi. *The Truce*, (1995) London: Abacus.

Levi, P. (1987) *I Sommersi e i salvati*, Torino: Einaudi. *The Drowned and the Saved*, (1988) London: Michael Joseph.

Lewis, C.S. (1992) *An Experiment in Criticism*, Cambridge: CUP.

Little, R., Redsell, P. and Wilcock, E. (1989) *GCSE Contexts*, London: Heinemann.

Marchant, T. (1994) *Speaking in Tongues*, broadcast by BBC Television on 22 July 1994.

Marenbon, J. (1987) *English our English: the new orthodoxy examined*, London: Centre for Policy Studies.

McCully, C. (1994) *The Poet's Voice and Craft*, Manchester: Carcanet.

140

Mill, J.S. (1873) *Autobiography.*

Miller, J.H. (1985) in *P.N. Review*, **48**.

Miller, J. (1986) *Subsequent Performances*, London: Faber and Faber.

Motion, A. (1994) *William Barnes: Selected Poems*, London: Penguin.

Muir, E. (1954) *An Autobiography*, London: Hogarth.

National Curriculum Council (1989) *English in the National Curriculum: a report to the Secretary of State for Education and Science on the statutory consultation for attainment targets and programmes of study in English at Key Stages 2, 3 and 4*, London: NCC.

National Curriculum Council (1990) *Core Skills*, London: NCC.

National Curriculum Council (1992) *National Curriculum English: The Case for Revising the Order: Advice to the Secretary of State for Education*, London: NCC.

National Curriculum Council (1993) *English in the National Curriculum: a report to the Secretary of State for Education and Science on the statutory consultation for attainment targets and programmes of study in English*, London: NCC.

Newbould, A. and Stibbs, A. (1983) *Exploring Texts through Reading Aloud and Dramatization*, London: Ward Lock.

Norman, K. (Ed.) (1992) *Thinking Voices – the work of the National Oracy Project*, London: Hodder and Stoughton.

Northern Examining Association (1986) *GCSE English Language.*

O'Malley, R. (1965) 'The missing word – a useful lesson' in B. Jackson (ed.) *English versus Examinations*, London: Chatto and Windus.

Office for Standards in Education (1995) *English: a review of inspection findings 1993/94*, London: HMSO.

Ong, W. (1967) *The Presence of the Word*, London: Yale University Press.

Orwell, G. (1960) *Selected Essays*, London: Penguin.

Orwell, S. and Angus, I. (1982) *The Collected Essays, Journalism and Letters of George Orwell: vol. 3 As I Please, 1943–1945*, London: Penguin.

Ousby, I. (1992) *The Cambridge Guide to Literature in English*, Cambridge: CUP.

Paulin, T. (Ed.) (1994) *The Faber Book of Vernacular Verse*, London: Penguin.

Pearsall Smith, L. (1943) *Words and Idioms*, London: Constable.

Pirrie, J. (1987) *On Common Ground: A Programme for Teaching Poetry*, London: Hodder and Stoughton.

Pirrie, J. (1993a) *Apple Fire: The Halesworth Middle School Anthology*, London: Bloodaxe Books.

Pirrie, J. (1993b) 'A Question of Balance', *The Use of English*, **45** (1), 1–16.

Pirrie, J. (1994) 'Learning to Reflect', *The Use of English*, **45** (2), 105–119.

Poole, R. and Shepherd, P. (1972) *Young Impact Three*, London: Heinemann Educational.

Quiller–Couch, A. (1920) *On the Art of Reading*, Cambridge: CUP.

Robinson, I. (1994) in *The Use of English* **45** (2) 166 – 170.

Rodenburg, P. (1993) *The Need for Words*, London: Methuen.

Roszak, T. (1986) *The Cult of Information*, Cambridge: Lutterworth Press.

Sacks, J. (1991) *The Reith Lectures: The Persistence of Faith: Religion, Morality and Society in a Secular Age*, London: Weidenfeld and Nicholson.

Sampson, G. (1970) *English for the English*, Cambridge: CUP.

Sarland, C. (1991) *Young People Reading: Culture and Response*, Milton Keynes: Open University Press.

Saunders, M., Hall, C. and Greenwood, S. (1993) *Focus on Fiction: New Approaches to Literature for Key Stage 4*, London: Heinemann.

School Examinations and Assessment Council (1990) *A Guide to Teacher Assessment – Pack C: A Source Book of Teacher Assessment*, London: SEAC.

School Examinations and Assessment Council (1991) *Children's Work Assessed: English Key Stage 1*, London: SEAC.

School Examinations and Assessment Council (1992) *Key Stage 3 Pupils' Work Assessed: English*, London: SEAC.

School Examinations and Assessment Council (1993) School Assessment folder, Sample Test Questions KS3, London: SEAC.

Secondary Examinations Council (1985) *Draft Grade Criteria for GCSE English*, London: SEC.

Secondary Examinations Council (1986) *English GCSE: A Guide for Teachers*, Milton Keynes: Open University Press.

Seely, J. and Kitchen, D. (1995) *The Heinemann English Programme 1*, London: Heinemann.

Shakespeare (1984) *Othello*, London: CUP.

Shattuck, R. (1984) *The Innocent Eye*, New York: Farrar Straus Giroux.

Smith, O. (1984) *The Politics of Language 1791–1819*, Oxford: Clarendon Press.

Stratta, L. Dixon, J. and Wilkinson A. (1973) *Patterns of Learning*, London: Heinemann.

Sutherland, G. (Ed.) (1973) *Arnold on Education*, London: Penguin.

Tate. N. (1994) 'Off the Fence on a Common Culture', *Times Educational Supplement*, 29 July 1994.

Taylor, M. (1993) *Exploring Language Change*, Cambridge: CUP.

Thomas, E. (1913) *Walter Pater*, A Critical Study.

Thomas, E. (1974) *Collected Poems*, London: Faber and Faber.

Thomas, E. (1993) *The South Country*, London: J.M. Dent.

Torbe, M. and Fry, D. (1990) *Poetry Readings*, London: Hodder and Stoughton.

Torbe, M. and Protherough, R. (Eds) (1977) *Classroom Encounters: Language and English Teaching*, London: Ward Lock/NATE.

Trilling, L. (1956) *The Portable Matthew Arnold*, New York: Viking.

Walker, T. (1982) *The High Path*, London: Routledge and Kegan Paul.

White, R.J. (1938) *The Political Thought of Samuel Taylor Coleridge: A Selection*, London: Cape.

Whitehead (1967) *The Aims of Education*, New York: Scribner.

Wordsworth, W. (1971) *The Prelude: a parallel text*, London: Penguin.

Index

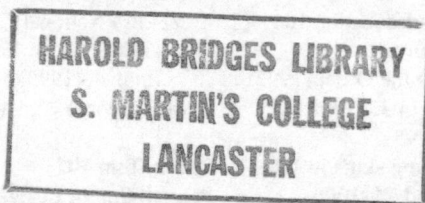